THE FARBERWARE®
CONVECTION TURBO-OVEN
COOKBOOK

by

Margaret Deeds Murphy

DORISON HOUSE PUBLISHERS/BOSTON

Acknowledgments

The author wishes to thank the following people at Farberware for their assistance, encouragement and double checking of recipes:

Kathy Cripps, Director, Product Information Center
Amy Christensen, Senior Home Economist

About the Author

Margaret Deeds Murphy, author and Home Economist, was born in Stromsburg, Nebraska, received her Home Economics degree from the University of Nebraska in 1937, and has been cooking, testing, and writing about food ever since. She is the author of a number of cookbooks, has been associated with several national magazines, was head of the Recipe Test Kitchens at General Foods Corporation as well as having her own consulting practice in New York City. Maggie, as she is known to her friends, lives with her husband on Cape Cod where she operates a test kitchen for the development of recipes and does food writing. She has prepared food pages for *Gray's Sporting Journal* and writes a weekly food column for the *Cape Cod Oracle* of Orleans, Massachusetts.

Copyright

ISBN: 0916752-44-5
Library of Congress Catalog Number: 78-72950
Manufactured in the United States of America

Eighth Printing, April 1986

Contents

introduction

Now that you own a convection oven you are well aware of the oven's assets. Convection ovens offer a unique combination of quality of cooking, savings of energy and time, safety and ease of operation and care.

Meats are juicier than ever and baked goods are picture perfect—all due to circulating hot air. Heat from a conventional electric element is fan-circulated to hit all sides of the food simultaneously, thus insuring even cooking.

Circulating air in the convection oven allows for other operations—like dehydrating, proofing, reheating and defrosting.

Dehydrating is the removal of moisture from food to retard spoilage. More in-depth information on dehydrating can be found in Chapter 9.

Professional bakeries use proofing rooms to allow their bread dough to rise to its fullest. Your convection oven is a "mini-proofing room." It can maintain a constant temperature of 90°F to allow your bread dough to proof (rise) like a professional baker. Specific proofing instructions can be found in Chapter 6.

Reheating of leftovers is easy in your Turbo-Oven. Left-overs can be reheated in oven safe casseroles or dishes or wrapped in foil. Set the temperature dial to 300°F or 350°F and heat until hot throughout. Reheating time will vary due to amount of food and type of food being reheated.

Defrosting in the convection oven can save you time. Place the frozen item on the rack and turn the temperature dial all the way down to its lowest temperature (this is marked with a dot). Air should not feel warm. Close the oven door and set the timer to "Stay On." Defrosting time varies with amount of food and type of food being defrosted.

Good cooking to you!

how the convection turbo-oven works

The Cooking Fan swirls heated air evenly around food in the Cooking Chamber. The Insulating Chamber keeps heat inside the oven. The Cooling Chamber Fan pulls kitchen air through the Outer Cooling Chamber so outside of oven stays cooler.

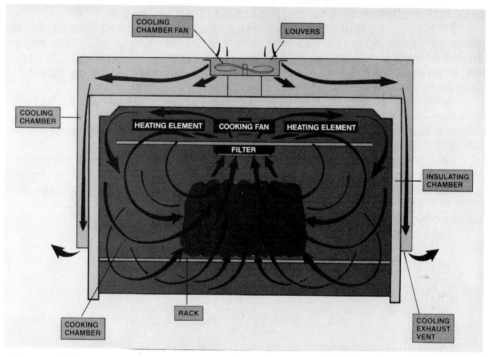

Courtesy of Farberware

Party Snacks

Nothing could be more convenient for producing party snacks than the convection oven. It works quickly, efficiently—acting as either an oven or a broiler to turn out appetizing "appeteazers" as one of my friends says.

Most party snacks can be prepared in advance and kept in the refrigerator or freezer until the party. If homemade party snacks are frozen, allow them to thaw slightly, then bake or broil as usual.

Commercially prepared frozen snacks should be cooked according to the package directions—just eliminate the oven preheating.

sausage-cheese biscuits

Mix the biscuit mix, sausage and cheese in advance and refrigerate. Add water and bake when ready to serve or bake early and reheat—400°F—5 minutes. These are also good when served cold.

1 1/2 cups buttermilk biscuit mix
3 sweet Italian sausages, skins removed
1 cup grated Cheddar cheese
1/2 cup water

With 2 knives or a pastry blender, mix biscuit mix, sausage and cheese until well blended. Stir in water to make a fairly stiff dough. Drop by teaspoons on an ungreased baking sheet. Bake at 300°F about 20 minutes. **Makes about 40.**

emerald puffs

The puff mixture can be prepared in advance and refrigerated, but don't put it on bread until just before broiling.

1 package (10-ounce) frozen, chopped spinach, defrosted
1/2 teaspoon grated nutmeg
1/2 cup chopped stuffed olives
1/2 cup grated Romano cheese
1 1/2 cups mayonnaise
Rye Party Bread

Squeeze all liquid from defrosted spinach. Mix with nutmeg, olives, cheese and mayonnaise. Spread on party bread rounds. Preheat oven to "BROIL" or 450°F for 10 minutes. Broil until bubbly. **Makes 36.**

bacon-onion pie

A tasty quiche-like party snack—can be prepared in advance and served at room temperature—or baked at the last minute and served hot. The filling can be put together ahead of time and refrigerated. Add to pie crust and bake before serving.

8 slices bacon, finely diced
4 medium (or 2 large) sweet Spanish onions, sliced thin
2 eggs
1 egg yolk
¾ cup dairy sour cream
1 teaspoon garlic salt
1 teaspoon paprika
1 unbaked 8-inch pie crust

Fry bacon until crisp. Remove bacon from skillet and drain off most of the fat. Add onions and cook slowly until tender. Beat eggs and egg yolk together and stir, with sour cream and seasoning into onions. Spoon into the pie crust. Sprinkle top with bacon. Bake at 350°F for 40 to 45 minutes. Cut into wedges and serve warm or cold. **Makes 6 to 8 servings.**

baked barbecued meatballs

The meatballs and sauce may be prepared separately early in the day, refrigerated and baked at serving time. They may also be completely cooked, refrigerated and reheated at serving time.

1 pound ground beef
4 tablespoons dry bread crumbs
1 egg, slightly beaten
$^1/_2$ teaspoon salt
$^1/_2$ teaspoon garlic powder
$^3/_4$ teaspoon onion powder

Mix all ingredients lightly and shape into 50 small meatballs. Preheat oven to "BROIL" or 450°F for 10 minutes. Put meatballs on drip tray and broil 5 to 10 minutes, until lightly browned. Pour off fat.

Sauce:

Combine **one 10$^1/_2$ ounce can tomato soup** with **5 tablespoons brown sugar, 3 tablespoons Worcestershire sauce, $^1/_4$ cup chopped onion, 2 tablespoons butter or margarine, 2 tablespoons vinegar,** and **1 tablespoon prepared mustard.** Simmer about 5 minutes. Pour over meatballs in pan and bake at 350°F for 30 minutes. Serve meatballs in a chafing dish. **Makes 50 meatballs.**

bacon twirls

These Bacon Twirls must be made in advance and baked at the last minute.

1 package (3-ounce) cream cheese
2 tablespoons cream
1 tablespoon chopped chives
6 slices fresh whole wheat bread, crusts removed
6 slices bacon

Soften cream cheese at room temperature. Combine with cream and chopped chives. Spread on one side of bread slices. Roll as in jelly roll. Wrap each roll in bacon. Chill. Cut into 3 to 4 slices. Bake at 400°F for 5 to 10 minutes or until bacon is crisp. **Makes 18 to 24.**

corned beef hash balls

This is one of those recipes called a "pantry shelfer." The ingredients can be kept on hand for a late call for party snacks. However, the hash balls can also be prepared, refrigerated, and ready to broil when needed, if planned for in advance.

1 can (1-pound) corned beef hash
1 tablespoon chopped onion
2 tablespoons catsup or chili sauce
1 tablespoon steak sauce
1 egg
1 tablespoon water
1 cup dry bread crumbs

Mix corned beef hash with onion, catsup and steak sauce. Shape into small balls. Mix egg and water. Dip balls in egg, then in crumbs. Place on drip tray. Preheat oven to "BROIL" or 450°F for 10 minutes. Broil corned beef hash balls 5 to 10 minutes, until hot and lightly browned. **Makes about 36 hash balls.**

oriental walnut munch mix

A good party snack which can be made several days in advance. Set bowls full of this snack in handy spots.

¼ cup soy sauce
¼ cup sugar
Few drops Tabasco sauce
10 cups rice chex
1 cup coarsely chopped walnuts

Blend soy sauce, sugar and Tabasco sauce. Mix rice chex and walnuts in a large bowl. Pour soy sauce mixture over and toss gently to blend. Spread in an ungreased 9 ×13-inch pan and bake at 250°F for 20 to 30 minutes, stirring occasionally. Cool. Store tightly covered to keep crisp. **Makes 10 cups.**

cheese squares

These tasty squares can be served warm or cold. They are gobbled up either way.

2 cups buttermilk biscuit mix
2 eggs, beaten
$^1/_2$ cup buttermilk
$^1/_2$ teaspoon crushed rosemary
$^1/_4$ cup melted butter or margarine
$^1/_2$ pound crumbled Feta or blue cheese

Combine biscuit mix with eggs, buttermilk and rosemary, mixing just until all flour is moistened. Spread into a well greased 13 ×9 ×2-inch pan. Pour butter over dough and sprinkle with cheese. Bake at 300°F for 35 to 40 minutes. Cool in pan. Cut into small squares. **Makes about 48 squares.**

ham-mushroom rollers

Ham-Mushroom Rollers can be prepared in advance, refrigerated and baked when ready to serve.

1 loaf (22-ounce) soft-textured white bread
1 can (10$^1/_2$-ounce) condensed cream of mushroom soup
Prepared mustard
$^1/_2$ pound thinly sliced cooked ham*

Remove crusts from bread slices. (Dry crusts in oven and use for dry bread crumbs.) Spread slices with soup. Roll as in jelly roll. Cut ham to fit length of bread. Spread ham with a little mustard. Wrap around bread roll. Fasten with toothpicks and cut in half crosswise. Bake about 10 minutes at 325°F. **Makes 48.**

---

*Bologna slices may be substituted.

quick party snacks

Pastry Devils:

Mix a **2-crust package pastry mix** with a **2½-ounce can deviled ham** and **2 to 3 tablespoons white wine.** Roll on floured board and cut into small squares or rounds. Sprinkle with **sesame seeds.** Bake at 400°F about 10 minutes. **Makes about 35.**

Crispy Bites:

Cut **frankfurters** in 1-inch pieces. Dip in **catsup** then roll in **crushed cornflake crumbs.** Place on greased baking sheet and bake at 350°F for 10 minutes or until hot.

Pantry Shelf Quick Trick:

Trim crusts from **9 slices of bread** and cut each into 4 squares. Spread lightly with **prepared mustard** and top each square with a dab of **drained pickle relish. Make 36 mounds** from a **1-pound can of corned beef hash** and place one on each bread square. Preheat oven at "BROIL" or 450°F for 10 minutes . Put squares on baking sheet and broil until heated through.

Pizza Shrimp:

Rinse and dry **tiny shrimp from a 5-ounce can.** Toss with ½ **cup grated American process cheese** and ⅓ **cup chopped parsley.** Spread over top of **1 large frozen pizza.** Heat as directed. Cut into squares to serve.

Kippers in Bacon:

Cut **kippers** crosswise into 1-inch pieces. Wrap each in ½ **slice bacon.** Fasten with toothpick. Preheat oven to "BROIL" or 450°F for 10 minutes. Broil on rack until bacon is crisp.

Hot Lobster:

Mix together **1 cup finely chopped, cooked lobster, dash Tabasco,** ½ **teaspoon each Worcestershire sauce** and **prepared mustard,** ¼ **cup mayonnaise.** Pile on 25 to 30 **Melba toast rounds.** Top with thin slices of **pimiento cheese.** Bake at 350°F for 5 minutes or until cheese is melted. **Makes 25 to 30.**

(continued on page 14)

(continued)

Fish Tidbits:

Cut **frozen fish sticks** into 3 pieces and heat as directed on package. Serve hot with **cocktail sauce.**

Cheese Sticks:

Toast **5 or 6 slices white bread.** Trim crusts and cut each into 5 strips. Dip in **melted butter** and place on baking sheet. Sprinkle with a mixture of ½ **cup cornflake crumbs** and **4 tablespoons grated Parmesan or Romano cheese.** Bake at 325°F for about 10 minutes or until lightly browned. **Makes about 30.**

Sesame Trick:

Butter **sesame wafers** with softened **garlic butter** and heat at 350°F for 5 minutes. Serve hot.

Cheese/Dairy/Vegetarian

Rising meat prices have many people searching for nutritious but tasty alternatives. The recipes from this chapter could be just the answer you need. Or perhaps you have your own meatless recipes—why not adapt them to the convection oven? Use the same temperatures you always do, but check for doneness five to ten minutes before the end of cooking time.

To save time and energy, plan to use the convection oven for an entire meal—perhaps a casserole, baked apples and biscuits.

Be sure to use your prettiest casserole dishes so that your meal can be brought right from the oven to the table. Anything that is oven-safe is perfect for the convection oven.

artichoke casserole

This elegant casserole when paired with buttered peas and a green salad spiked with orange slices makes a lovely meal.

1 can (8½-ounce) artichoke hearts, drained and sliced in half
3 hard-cooked eggs, sliced
½ cup sliced green olives
¼ cup sliced water chestnuts
1 can (10½-ounce) condensed chicken soup
¼ cup milk
½ cup grated American cheese
½ cup buttered bread crumbs

Arrange artichokes in a buttered shallow casserole. Add a layer of eggs, olives and water chestnuts. Mix soup with milk and pour over casserole. Top with cheese and crumbs. Bake at 350°F until bubbly and crumbs are browned, about 20 minutes. **Makes 4 servings.**

mushroom-cheese soufflé

This soufflé is as beautiful as it is good. But soufflés won't wait for the diners — so eat it when ready.

2 tablespoons butter or margarine
1 small onion, grated
1 cup chopped fresh mushrooms
1 can (10½-ounce) condensed cream of mushroom soup
¼ teaspoon dried rosemary
2 cups shredded natural American cheese
6 eggs, separated

Heat butter in a saucepan and sauté onion and mushrooms over low heat until mushrooms are dry. Stir in soup, rosemary (if leaf rosemary, pulverize with mortar and pestle) and cheese. Beat egg whites until stiff, beat egg yolks until light and fluffy. Fold egg yolks into mushroom soup and gently fold in egg whites. Spoon into a buttered 2½-quart soufflé dish. Bake at 375°F for 30 to 40 minutes. Serve at once. **Makes 4 servings.**

rice and lentil casserole

The addition of cheese to the casserole makes it a substitute for meat. Baked carrots and cole slaw could complete the menu.

1 cup rice
¾ cup dried lentils
¼ cup butter
1 cup diced celery
1 cup diced onion
1 can (16 ounces) tomatoes
1 teaspoon curry powder
1 teaspoon sugar
1 teaspoon salt
1 cup grated Cheddar cheese
½ cup buttered bread crumbs

Wash rice and lentils and cook together in boiling water 15 to 20 minutes. Drain. Heat butter and sauté celery and onion until soft but not browned. Add tomatoes, seasonings and mix with drained rice and lentils. Layer in a buttered 2-quart casserole with cheese. Sprinkle buttered bread crumbs on top and bake at 300°F for 30 minutes or until bubbly. Let stand about 5 minutes before serving. **Makes 4 to 6 servings.**

manicotti

Manicotti, seemingly, has as many recipes as cooks. All agree to some extent to the filling, but the "case" for the filling can be crêpes (pancake-like rounds), homemade pasta dough or purchased pasta for manicotti. However it is done, it is a delicious dish of Italian origin. While it is baking, add Italian bread to be heated. Serve with a big green salad and spumoni for dessert.

Pasta Pancakes

3 eggs
1 cup all-purpose flour
$1/8$ teaspoon salt
1 cup water

Put eggs in bowl and beat with whisk until light. Add flour gradually, beating until batter is smooth after each addition. Add salt and beat in water gradually. Heat a crêpe skillet or an 8-inch skillet. Brush with oil and put 2 tablespoons of batter into skillet and spread with spoon to form round. Cook over medium heat 1 minute. Pasta should not brown. Do not turn. Remove from skillet to wax paper. **Continue to make 16.** Cover and hold until ready to fill.

Filling

$1/2$ pound ricotta cheese
$1/4$ pound mozzarella cheese, cut in small cubes
1 ounce Parmesan cheese, grated
1 egg
2 tablespoons chopped parsley
$1/2$ teaspoon salt
Freshly ground pepper to taste

Combine all ingredients and mix to blend well.

To assemble:

Divide cheese mixture among 16 manicotti pasta, placing down center of pasta pancake on the uncooked side. Roll like a cigar and place, seam side down, in a buttered flat casserole, large enough so that the manicotti is in a single layer. Cover with Tomato Sauce. Bake at 350°F until hot and bubbly, about 30 minutes. **Makes 4 to 6 servings.** An additional strip of mozarella may be put over the sauce before baking, if desired.

Notes: The manicotti can be assembled in advance and refrigerated until ready to cook. Add Tomato Sauce and add about 10 minutes to cooking time.
    If commercially prepared manicotti shells are used, cook as directed and fill with cheese mixture.

Tomato Sauce

¼ cup olive oil
1 medium onion, finely chopped
1 clove garlic, finely chopped
2 cups canned Italian crushed tomatoes
1 can (6-ounce) tomato paste
1 cup water
½ teaspoon salt
½ teaspoon sugar
2 tablespoons chopped fresh basil or 1 tablespoon dried basil, crushed

Heat oil and cook onion and garlic until lightly browned. Add remaining ingredients. Bring to a boil and simmer, covered, about 1 hour stirring occasionally. **Makes 4 cups.**

lentil-lima bean meatless loaf

Creamed carrots and Waldorf apple salad could be teamed with the loaf.

1 cup dried lima beans
1 cup dried lentils
Water
$1/2$ teaspoon salt
Freshly ground pepper to taste
1 cup salted peanuts, finely chopped
$1/2$ cup finely chopped onion
$1/4$ cup finely chopped green pepper
1 cup soft bread crumbs
2 tablespoons chopped parsley
2 tablespoons melted butter or margarine
2 eggs
$1/2$ cup milk
3 tablespoons melted butter or margarine
$1/4$ cup hot water

Wash beans and lentils and soak in water to cover for several hours. Bring to a boil and simmer until tender. Drain and process in food processer or blender until smooth. Put into a bowl and add remaining ingredients except for 3 tablespoons melted butter and $1/4$ cup hot water, mixing well. Spoon into a greased and floured 9 ×4-inch loaf pan. Bake at 300°F about 45 minutes or until firm. Baste several times during the last 15 minutes with butter mixed with hot water. **Makes 8 servings.**

eggplant casserole

Eggplant Casserole will form the basis for a good meal. With it serve buttered natural rice, a salad of garbanzo beans, chopped onions and herbs.

1 medium eggplant (about ½ pound)
1 cup dry bread crumbs (about)
1 egg beaten
2 tablespoons water
4 tablespoons olive oil
Salt and freshly ground pepper to taste
1 onion, sliced
2 cups canned tomatoes
1 teaspoon sugar
¼ pound thinly sliced mozzarella cheese*

Peel and slice eggplant into ¼-inch thick slices. Dip slices in bread crumbs, then in egg mixed with water and again in crumbs. Heat half the oil in a 10-inch skillet and quickly sauté half the slices on both sides. Add remaining oil to skillet and brown remaining eggplant slices. As browned, layer into a buttered 8 ×8-inch square or oblong baking pan. Sprinkle with salt and pepper to taste. Add onion slices to skillet and sauté until lightly browned, stirring. Arrange over eggplant. Heat tomatoes and sugar in skillet in which eggplant and onion were fried and pour over eggplant. Arrange mozarella slices on top. Bake at 375°F for 20 minutes or until hot and bubbly. **Makes 4 servings.**

---

*¾ cup grated Parmesan cheese can be substituted for mozarella slices. It bakes with a crispy cheese crust.

red beans pueblo

A big bowl of cole slaw and hot cornbread would enhance Red Beans Pueblo.

1 tablespoon vegetable oil
1 small onion, chopped
$\frac{1}{2}$ green pepper, chopped
1 tablespoon Worcestershire sauce
2 teaspoons chili powder
4 cups cooked red kidney beans
$\frac{1}{4}$ pound American cheese, grated

Heat oil and sauté onion and green pepper until tender. Mix with seasonings and beans. Spoon into a buttered 5-cup casserole and sprinkle with grated cheese. Bake at 350°F for 25 minutes or until bubbly. **Makes 4 servings.**

tasty limas

This is a plan-ahead recipe, but well worth it. Accompany this dish with a salad of chopped lettuce spiked with banana and pineapple chunks.

2 cups dried lima beans
6 cups cold water
1 small onion, sliced
$\frac{1}{4}$ cup butter or margarine
$1\frac{1}{2}$ tablespoons Dijon style mustard
2 teaspoons steak sauce
$1\frac{1}{2}$ teaspoons chili powder
1 teaspoon salt
1 can ($10\frac{1}{2}$-ounce) condensed tomato soup
5 tablespoons cider vinegar

Sort and wash beans. Soak overnight in the 6 cups water. In the morning bring to a boil and boil 2 minutes. Remove from heat and let stand 1 hour. Then simmer beans slowly for about 30 minutes or until tender. Drain. Reserve liquid. Combine remaining ingredients with $1\frac{1}{2}$ cups bean liquid. Stir in beans and spoon into a 2-quart casserole. Bake at 350°F about 60 minutes. **Makes 6 servings.**

broccoli casserole

Broccoli Casserole makes a nice light luncheon main dish. Serve toasted rolls and a mixed fruit salad with it.

1 package (10-ounce) frozen broccoli spears
4 hard cooked eggs
Freshly ground pepper to taste
1 can (10½-ounce) condensed Cheddar cheese soup
4 tablespoons milk
¼ cup buttered crumbs

Cook broccoli as directed on package. Drain. Arrange in a 9-inch pie plate, stems toward center. Slice eggs and layer over broccoli. Sprinkle with pepper to taste. Mix soup and milk and spoon over eggs and broccoli. Sprinkle buttered crumbs over sauce. Bake at 375°F for 20 minutes or until bubbly and brown. **Makes 4 servings.**

rice and cheese custard

This is a beautiful casserole for a meatless day. Tomato halves sprinkled with seasoned salt and dabbed with butter and French rolls can go into the oven the last 15 minutes.

2 medium onions, chopped
2 stalks celery, chopped
¼ cup butter or margarine
1½ cups milk
3 eggs, slightly beaten
1 teaspoon salt
1 teaspoon Worcestershire sauce
½ cup chopped parsley
2 cups shredded Cheddar cheese
2 cups cooked rice
½ cup buttered crumbs

Sauté onions and celery in butter until tender, not browned. Mix with milk, eggs, salt, Worcestershire sauce and parsley. Blend with cheese and rice. Spoon into a buttered 1½-quart casserole. Top with crumbs. Bake at 350°F 30 minutes or until bubbly and browned. **Makes 4 to 6 servings.**

vegetable melange

Start the menu with cream of mushroom soup. Serve brown rice with the vegetable melange. Bake apples for dessert while the casserole is baking.

1 eggplant (1 pound) peeled and cubed
1 tablespoon salt
1 small clove garlic, finely chopped
1 small onion, finely chopped
2 tablespoons butter or margarine
$\frac{1}{4}$ cup chopped green pepper
2 cups bread cubes
2 cups corn cut off the cob
4 tablespoons butter or margarine
3 eggs
2 teaspoons Dijon style mustard
$\frac{1}{2}$ teaspoon Italian seasoning
Freshly ground pepper to taste
1 cup milk
2 large ripe tomatoes, sliced
$\frac{1}{4}$ cup bread crumbs

In a large bowl combine eggplant and salt. Let stand 5 or 10 minutes, then drain. Sauté garlic and onion in 2 tablespoons butter until tender, not browned. Spoon into a large bowl and add green pepper and bread and mix well. Sauté eggplant and corn in 4 tablespoons butter until lightly browned. Add to onion mixture and toss together. Spoon into a buttered 2-quart casserole. Combine eggs with seasonings and milk and pour over vegetables. Top with tomato slices and bake, covered, at 350°F for 40 minutes. Sprinkle crumbs over casserole and bake, uncovered, 10 minutes longer. **Makes 6 servings.**

tomato-cheese casserole

Sliced pears on chopped lettuce with cranberry sauce and hot muffins served with the casserole will round out this meal.

$1/2$ **cup sliced stuffed olives**
$3/4$ **cup thinly sliced green onions**
3 slices Muenster cheese
$1/4$ **cup flour**
$1/2$ **teaspoon salt**
Freshly ground pepper to taste
2 large ripe tomatoes
2 tablespoons butter or margarine
2 eggs, beaten
1 cup milk
1 cup grated Cheddar cheese
Chopped fresh parsley

Mix olives and onions and spoon into the bottom of a buttered $8 \times 8 \times 2$-inch pan. Top with Muenster cheese. Mix flour with salt and pepper. Slice tomatoes into $1/2$-inch thick slices and dip in flour mixture. Sauté quickly on both sides in butter and add to casserole. (If there is any flour mixture left, sprinkle it on the tomatoes in the casserole.) Mix eggs with milk and Cheddar cheese and pour over tomatoes. Bake at 350°F for 45 minutes or until filling is set. Sprinkle with chopped parsley. **Makes 4 to 6 servings.**

potato-carrot-cheese bake

A healthful combination of foods. Asparagus tips, lettuce wedges with a tart dressing and some hot bread for a complete menu.

4 tablespoons butter or margarine
1 small onion, minced
4 tablespoons flour
3 cups milk
2 tablespoons Dijon style mustard
$^1/_2$ teaspoon salt
1 cup grated American cheese
6 medium potatoes
3 large carrots
$^3/_4$ cup buttered crumbs

Heat butter in saucepan and sauté onion until tender but not browned. Add flour and mix well. Stir in milk and cook and stir until mixture is thickened. Fold in mustard, salt and cheese. Peel potatoes and carrots and slice thinly. In a 2-quart shallow casserole, layer potatoes, carrots and sauce, ending with sauce. Top with crumbs. Bake at 350°F for 1 hour or until potatoes are tender. **Makes 4 to 6 servings.**

cottage cheese

You can make your own cottage cheese and the convection oven is the perfect place to start it.

2²/₃ cups nonfat dry milk powder*
2 quarts cold water
¹/₂ cup buttermilk
¹/₄ cup milk
¹/₂ teaspoon salt

Combine milk powder, water and buttermilk in a 3-quart stainless steel or enamel-lined metal bowl. Cover tightly and place in oven. Set the temperature control dial between the "1" and the "5" of the 150°F setting or between the end of the black line and the 150°F setting. Air should feel warm not hot. Allow to stay in oven 6 to 8 hours. The milk should be set solidly. In a 4-quart saucepan add 2 cups water. Bring to a boil, reduce heat so water simmers; put pan with milk into the water. Let stand 15 minutes, stirring once every 5 minutes. The milk should form into curds which separate from the whey. If you prefer a soft cottage cheese, remove from water and strain cheese through cheesecloth put inside colander. If your preference is for a cheese with more of a curd, let milk "cook" a little longer. Put strained cheese in a small bowl and stir in about ¹/₄ cup milk and ¹/₂ teaspoon salt. Cheese should be stored, covered in the refrigerator. It will keep about 10 days. **Makes about 1 pint.**

---

*2 quarts of whole milk or nonfat milk may be used in place of dry milk powder and water.

yogurt

This is a low-calorie plain yogurt. The texture is a little less creamy than plain yogurt purchased at the store, but it is very good. Serve with fruit or preserves, if you desire.

2²/₃ cups nonfat dry milk powder
7¹/₃ cups boiling water
4 tablespoons plain yogurt starter*

Mix milk powder and boiling water in a bowl and let cool to room temperature. In each of 4 pint jars, put a tablespoon of yogurt. Add milk and give each jar a gentle stir. Cover with the lids and put in the convection oven. Set the temperature control dial between the "1" and the "5" of the 150°F setting or between the end of the black line and the 150°F setting. Set timer to STAY ON. It will take about 6 to 8 hours for the yogurt to set. Start checking at 5 to 5¹/₂ hours. Refrigerate at once. **Makes 4 pints.**

***Notes:** For the first batch you will need commercial yogurt. After that, save enough of your own to continue making the yogurt. Any glass jars will do as long as the proportion of yogurt to 1 pint milk is observed. Half the recipe can be prepared by following the directions on the dry milk carton for 1 quart milk and using 2 tablespoons yogurt.

A lower temperature will take longer to set the yogurt.

Meats/Stews/Casseroles

Roasted and broiled meats are juicier and more succulent when prepared in the convection oven. Cook directly on the rack so that the heated moving air surrounds the meat on all sides, sealing in the natural juices and cutting roasting time. Broiled meats do not have to be turned.

To broil set the temperature dial to "BROIL" or 450°F and preheat the oven for 10 minutes. Put refrigerator temperature meat directly on the rack. Broiling time in the convection oven is about the same as in a conventional oven.

Roasting in the convection oven is done at the same temperatures you've always used but in ⅓ less the time. Therefore a turkey that took 3 hours at 300°F in your ordinary oven will take only 2 hours at 300°F in your convection oven!

Besides reducing roasting time you can also save energy by preparing the rest of the meal at the same time. Baked potatoes and a vegetable casserole would go nicely with a roast beef.

In this chapter are recipes to use your convection as a slow cooker with the temperature set at 225°F and the timer set at the STAY ON position; the convection oven functions as a slow cooker, eliminating another piece of equipment in the kitchen.

roasting chart

VARIETY OF MEAT WITH OVEN TEMP.	CUT	WEIGHT IN POUNDS	APPROX. ROASTING TIME*	FROZEN MEATS APPROX. ROASTING TIME	INTERNAL TEMP. AT END OF ROASTING TIME	
BEEF ROAST 300°F	Standing Rib	3-6	18-23 min/lb 24-28 min/lb 29-34 min/lb	27-33 min/lb 32-38 min/lb 39-45 min/lb	rare med well	110°-120° 130°-140° 150°-160°
	Standing Rib	7-10	14-18 min/lb 19-23 min/lb 24-29 min/lb	23-28 min/lb 28-33 min/lb 34-39 min/lb	rare med well	110°-120° 130°-140° 150°-160°
	Rib Roast, boned and tied	3-6	17-23 min/lb 24-30 min/lb 31-37 min/lb	35-40 min/lb 41-47 min/lb 47-51 min/lb	rare med well	110°-120° 130°-140° 150°-160°
	Sirloin Tip, tied	4-7	14-17 min/lb 18-21 min/lb 22-25 min/lb	22-30 min/lb 30-38 min/lb 38-45 min/lb	rare med well	110°-120° 130°-140° 150°-160°
	Eye Round	3-6	15-18 min/lb 19-23 min/lb 24-28 min/lb	22-27 min/lb 27-32 min/lb 32-37 min/lb	rare med well	110°-120° 130°-140° 150°-160°
FRESH PORK 300°F	Loin, bone-in	3-7	26-33 min/lb	43-48 min/lb	well	170°
	Loin, boned and tied	3-5	20-30 min/lb	38-43 min/lb	well	170°
	Picnic Shoulder	5-8	29-34 min/lb	43-48 min/lb	well	170°
	Fresh Ham	3-7	26-33 min/lb	43-48 min/lb	well	170°
SMOKED PORK 300°F	Half Ham, fully cooked	5-7	16-20 min/lb			140°
	Whole Ham, fully cooked	10-14	12-17 min/lb			140°
	Picnic Shoulder, fully cooked	5-8	15-20 min/lb			140°
LAMB 300°F	Leg Of Lamb	3-8	20-25 min/lb 25-35 min/lb	25-35 min/lb 35-45 min/lb	med well	140°-150° 170°
VEAL 300°F	Veal Shoulder, rolled	4-7	30-45 min/lb	42-47 min/lb	well	170°

*Note: Meat should be at refrigerator temperature.

broiling chart

VARIETY OF MEAT WITH OVEN TEMP.	CUT	WEIGHT OR THICKNESS	APPROX. BROILING TIME IN MINUTES*		FROZEN MEATS APPROX. BROILING TIME IN MINUTES	
BEEF "BROIL" or 450°F	Club, Rib, Flank or Shell Steak	1 inch	rare	10-13	rare	20-22
			med	14-18	med	23-25
	Sirloin or Porterhouse Steak	1 inch	rare	14-18	rare	28-32
			med	19-24	med	33-38
	Chuck Steak	1 inch	rare	13-16	rare	22-25
			med	17-20	med	26-30
	Hamburger	1 inch (4 oz)	rare	12-14	rare	22-25
			med	15-18	med	26-29
		1 inch (8 oz)	rare	15-19	rare	30-33
			med	20-24	med	35-38
	Liver	1/2 inch	med	6-8		
			well	8-10		
	Frankfurters	1 lb		5-8		
PORK "BROIL" or 450°F	Chops: Loin, Rib, Tenderloin	3/4 inch	well	19-23	well	23-25
	Ham Slice, fully cooked	3/4 inch		12		
	Bacon	8-10 slices		5-8		
	Sausage Patties	1/4-1/2 inch				12-15
	Brown 'N Serve Sausage	8-oz pkg				6-8
LAMB "BROIL" or 450°F	Chops: Rib, Loin, Shoulder	1 inch	med	15-18	med	18-24
			well	19-23		
VEAL "BROIL" or 450°F	Chops: Loin, Rib	1 inch		15-18		

*Note: Meat should be at refrigerator temperature.

ALL TIMES ARE BASED ON A PREHEATED OVEN.

crown roast of lamb

One of the most elegant meats you can cook is Crown Roast of Lamb. It is at least two rib sections (racks) of lamb shaped together to look like a crown. The butcher "Frenches" or scrapes the meat off the rib ends. When the roast is finished and the rib ends are decorated with paper frills or large stuffed olives, it truly becomes a crown.

Our roast is stuffed with a mixture made of the ground trimmings plus a little additional lamb. However, the crown can be stuffed with any dressing you choose, or roasted unstuffed. If the latter, roast upside down (the Frenched rib ends on the bottom). Invert and fill with vegetables. To carve, slice down between chops, cutting out one chop at a time and a portion of the lamb mixture.

We cooked wild rice in the oven at the same time as the lamb was cooking. The rest of the menu included asparagus spears, sliced orange and onion salad, mint jelly, hot rolls, (baked after the lamb was taken from the oven) and the Apple Pie Torte .

2 pounds ground lamb
1 medium size green pepper,
    finely chopped
1 medium size onion, finely
    chopped
1 can (3-ounce) sliced mushrooms
¾ cup fine dry bread crumbs

2 eggs, beaten
2 teaspoons salt
Freshly ground pepper to taste
Bacon
1 crown roast of lamb (5 to 6
    pounds) containing 2 whole
    rib sections

Combine ground lamb with vegetables, bread crumbs, eggs, salt and pepper and mix to blend well. Protect rib ends with pieces of salt pork or bacon wrapped around ends and then covered with aluminum foil. Put crown roast on a piece of heavy duty foil large enough to just bring up around the base of the roast. Fill center with ground lamb mixture. Position roast on one side of rack set over drip tray in lowest position in oven. Set probe temperature dial between 150-170°F depending on doneness desired. Insert probe into outlet and into lamb, being certain not to hit bone or fat. Set temperature dial at 300°F and the on/off timer to STAY ON. Allow approximately 20 to 25 minutes per pound. When roast is cooked, let stand 15 minutes before carving. Remove foil on rib ends and garnish with paper frills or large stuffed olives. A roast this size should serve 6 to 8 people. If desired, garnish roast with canned crab apples.

WILD RICE CASSEROLE

Put 1½ cups wild rice in a 6-cup casserole. Add 4 cups boiling water, 4 tablespoons butter, 5 chicken bouillon cubes and stir well. Cover and put in oven at same time as lamb. Stir again before serving. Makes 6-8 servings.

Note: If your convection oven does not have a Probe-A-Matic Control, insert a meat thermometer in roast, avoiding bone and fat, and roast to same temperature (150–170°F) at 300°F, approximately 20 to 25 minutes per pound.

roast eye round with red wine sauce

Roast beef with the Red Wine Sauce will make a good starting point for the menu. Add the Swedish Potatoes, baked at the same time, some broccoli and crisp celery.

1 (3 pounds) eye round beef roast
salt and freshly ground pepper

Red Wine Sauce:

2 cups dry red wine
4 green onions, chopped
2 cloves garlic, minced
2 tablespoons butter or margarine
2 tablespoons lemon juice
2 tablespoons chopped parsley
Salt and freshly ground pepper to taste

Put beef eye round on rack over drip tray at floor position. Rub with salt and pepper. Set probe temperature dial to 140°F for medium rare—lower for rare, higher for well done. Insert probe into roast being sure not to hit a pocket of fat. Insert connection into wall, set oven temperature at 300°F and timer to STAY ON. A roast this size will take about 1½ hours to reach medium rare. While roast is baking, combine wine, onions, and garlic and boil until reduced one-half. Add remaining ingredients, seasoning to taste. **Makes about 1 cup.** Let roast stand 10–15 minutes before carving. Serve sliced with Red Wine Sauce. **Makes 6 servings.**

Broccoli

Trim **broccoli** and put in a casserole with ½ **cup water, 2 tablespoons butter** and **salt** to taste. Add **2 tablespoons lemon juice**, if desired, cover and cook at 300°F for 45 minutes.

Note: If your oven does not have a Probe-A-Matic Control, set temperature at 300°F, timer at 1¼ hours, allowing about 20 minutes per pound for medium rare or 140°F on meat thermometer.

broiled wine burgers

Heat twice baked potatoes and cook wine burgers at the same time. The wine added to the ground beef keeps the burgers flavorful and moist.

1½ pounds ground beef
1 teaspoon salt
5–6 tablespoons dry red wine
Freshly grated pepper to taste
1 small onion, grated

Lightly mix all ingredients and shape into 4 to 6 thick (1-inch thick) patties. Preheat at "BROIL" or 450°F for 10 minutes without drip tray and rack. Put burgers on rack over drip pan and insert at floor level. At the same time put in twice baked potatoes. Broil burgers 12 to 14 minutes for rare to medium. **Makes 4 to 6 servings.**

quick tamale pie

This hearty casserole is a favorite for fall football parties. Heat mixed vegetables in a covered casserole and rolls in the oven while the Tamale Pie is baking. Add cole slaw to complete the menu.

½ cup cold water
½ cup cornmeal
1½ cups boiling water
½ teaspoon salt
2 cans (16-ounce) pork and beans with tomato sauce
½ pound ground beef
4 ripe olives, chopped
1 tablespoon instant onion
1 teaspoon chili powder

Combine cold water and cornmeal. Add to boiling water and salt. Cook and stir until thickened. Cover and cook over low heat 10 minutes. Set aside. Combine beans with remaining ingredients and heat. Spoon into a flat (10 ×6 ×2-inch) baking dish. Top with cornmeal. Bake at 350°F for 30 minutes or until cornmeal crust is browned. **Makes 4 to 6 servings.**

gravy for roast beef

This gravy can be made in advance, reheated, and the pan juices added when ready to serve.

3 fresh mushrooms, sliced
1 tablespoon butter or margarine
½ cup dry red wine
1 can (10¼-ounce) beef gravy
Pan juices

Sauté mushrooms in butter for 2 to 3 minutes in a small skillet. Add wine and boil until wine is almost evaporated. Stir in beef gravy and bring to a boil. If there are any pan juices from roast (not fat), stir into gravy. Serve hot with roast beef. **Makes 1½ cups.**

wine marinated steak

The wine marinade gives a fine flavor to the steak and helps tenderize the meat. Cut the steak in thin slices to serve.

2 cups dry red wine
½ cup vegetable oil
¼ cup lemon juice
1 medium onion, sliced
6 whole peppercorns, crushed
Several sprigs of parsley
1 small bay leaf
1 or 2 sprigs fresh thyme or ½ teaspoon dried
2 pounds boneless beef chuck steak, or beef chuck London broil

Combine wine with oil, lemon juice, onion and seasonings in a flat dish. Put steak into marinade and let stand 4 or 5 hours or overnight in the refrigerator, turning occasionally. When ready to cook, remove drip tray and rack from oven and preheat to "BROIL" (450°F) for 10 minutes. Place steak on rack and broil about 12 minutes. (If steak is more than 1½-inches thick, it can be broiled with the probe inserted so that it does not touch fat or bone. Set probe dial temperature at 115°F (rare), oven temperature at "BROIL" and timer at STAY ON.) Both the time and temperature given for cooking this steak will produce a steak on the rare side. The less expensive cuts of steak are better when not overcooked. **Makes 4 servings.**

Note: Save leftover marinade in refrigerator and reuse. It will keep for several weeks.

kebabs

Kebabs are a very good way in which to stretch the meat budget. They can be made with lamb, beef, veal or pork, but also with meat balls, thick pieces of raw chicken or turkey as well as fish and shellfish.

For added flavor the meat can be marinated, but if the meat is a tender cut this is not essential. Allow about ¼ pound meat per person.

The meats should be skewered with vegetables and/or fruits to enhance the flavor of both as the kebab is cooked.

Follow the instructions for broiling, preheating the oven as directed. Place the kebabs directly on the rack over drip tray and broil, without turning, for 8 to 10 minutes. Pork may require a little longer cooking.

Here are some suggestions for combinations:

Beef–Veal–Lamb

Green pepper squares
Small onions, parboiled or thick onion slices
Thick slices of zucchini squash
Tomato wedges or cherry tomatoes
Eggplant cubes
Canned potatoes
Mushroom caps
Chunks of carrots, parboiled

Pork

Any of the above plus:

Pineapple cubes
Large stuffed olives
Chunks of banana
Parboiled sweet potato chunks

Liver can also be used in a kebab. String chunks of baby beef or calf liver between pieces of partially cooked bacon, and broil for 8 to 10 minutes.

Here are two marinades:
Red Wine-Tomato Sauce:

1 cup tomato juice
1/4 cup chopped green pepper
1 small onion, chopped
1/2 cup vegetable oil
2 cloves pressed garlic
2 teaspoons chili powder
1/2 cup dry red wine
2 tablespoons wine vinegar

Combine all ingredients and mix well. Add meat and marinate 4 hours or overnight, turning occasionally. **Makes 2 1/2 cups.**

White Wine Sauce:

1 cup chablis wine
1/2 cup vegetable oil
1 onion, sliced
1 teaspoon salt
Freshly ground pepper to taste
1/2 teaspoon each thyme, rosemary and marjoram

Combine all ingredients and mix well. Add meat and marinate 4 hours or overnight, turning occasionally. **Makes 1 1/2 cups.**

liver in wine sauce

Fluffy mashed potatoes, buttered green beans and baked spiced applesauce (pg 94) could finish this menu.

1¼ pounds sliced calf or baby beef liver
4 tablespoons butter or margarine
¼ teaspoon thyme
1 tablespoon chopped parsley
2 teaspoons prepared mustard
¼ teaspoon salt
⅓ cup heavy cream
2 tablespoons dry white wine
Freshly ground pepper to taste

Brown liver lightly in butter. As slices are browned, transfer to a flat, buttered casserole. When all liver is browned, add remaining ingredients to skillet and stir over low heat to get browned butter from skillet bottom. Pour over liver in casserole. Bake at 350°F for 10 to 15 minutes. **Makes 4 servings.**

baked lentils and sausage

A salad of sliced oranges and cottage cheese would be good with this casserole. Heat some Sourdough Bread (pg. 87) when the casserole is baking.

½ pound dried lentils (3½ cups cooked)
Water
2 tablespoons butter or margarine
1 cup coarsely chopped onion
1 cup coarsely chopped celery
½ teaspoon salt
Freshly ground pepper to taste
½ pound Keilbasa sausage

Wash lentils. Cover with water to about 3 inches above lentils and simmer 20 minutes. Heat butter and saute onion and celery 5 minutes over moderate heat. Combine with lentils, salt and pepper and spoon into a buttered 6-cup casserole. Remove skin from Keilbasa and slice into thin slices. Tuck into the lentils in casserole. Bake at 300°F for about 45 minutes. If needed, add additional water during baking. **Makes 4 servings.**

ham slice with wine glaze

Put 4 medium-size yams in to bake at 300°F about 15 minutes before the ham slice. Tuck the Vegetable Package in the oven with the ham slice, and voila! Dinner is in the oven.

1-inch center cut ham slice
Cloves
½ cup orange marmalade
¼ cup dry white wine

Put ham slice in a buttered flat pan. Stick with cloves. Mix marmalade and wine and pour over ham slice. Bake at 300°F about 45 minutes or until lightly browned. Baste several times. **Makes 4 servings.**

Vegetable Package:

Wash, trim and slice **1 pound green beans** into 1-inch pieces. Place on an 18 × 16-inch rectangle of heavy duty foil. Peel and chop **1 ripe tomato** over the beans. Sprinkle with **salt, freshly ground pepper** and **dried rosemary**. Cut up **½ cup celery** and sprinkle over beans. Add **2 tablespoons butter or margarine.** Bring foil up around mixture and seal tightly. Bake in oven 45 minutes at 300°F. Open and toss together **to serve 4.**

roast fresh pork butt with onion sauce

Potatoes could be baked while the pork is cooking. Biscuits could go in on a second rack.

1 fresh pork butt, about 4 pounds
Salt and freshly ground pepper

Onion Sauce:

---

4 medium onions
1 cup water
1 tablespoon butter or margarine
1 tablespoon flour
2 tablespoons lemon juice
2 tablespoons vinegar
Salt and freshly ground pepper

Put pork butt on rack over drip tray in floor position. Rub with salt and pepper. Set probe temperature dial to 170°F. Insert probe into pork, being sure not to hit a bone or a pocket of fat. Insert connection into oven wall. Set oven temperature at 300°F and timer to STAY ON. Roast should take about 2¼ hours.* While roast is baking, prepare onion sauce as follows: Cook onions covered in water until very tender. Purée, with liquid, in blender or food processor. Heat butter and flour together in a saucepan. Add puréed onions, lemon juice, vinegar and cook and stir until mixture boils. Season to taste. **Makes about 2 cups.** Let roast stand 10 to 15 minutes before serving. Serve sliced pork with onion sauce. **Makes 6 servings.**

*Note: If your oven does not have a Probe-A-Matic Control, set temperature at 300°F, timer at 2¼ hours, allowing about 30 minutes per pound or 170°F on meat thermometer, inserted to miss bone and fat pockets.

stuffed pork chops

Stuffed pork chops, broccoli, chilled apple sauce and hot bread make the main course of this meal.

2 thick loin pork chops*
¾ cup soft bread crumbs
2 tablespoons melted butter
1 tablespoon chopped fresh parsley
1 tablespoon chopped onion
1 teaspoon whole peppercorns, crushed
1 teaspoon prepared mustard
1 teaspoon prepared horseradish
¼ teaspoon salt

*Have butcher cut a pocket in each pork chop for stuffing. Trim off excess fat. Mix remaining ingredients together lightly and stuff into pocket. Secure opening with skewers. Place rack in bottom position over drip pan. Put pork chops on one side of rack. Bake at 375°F for 40 minutes. Ten minutes before pork chops are done, add some foil wrapped bread to heat if desired.
Makes 2 servings.

Brocolli Spears For Two:

Trim **broccoli** and put in a casserole with **salt and pepper** to taste and with **2 tablespoons of butter** and **3 tablespoons of water**. Place in oven with pork chops during last ½ hour of cooking.

barbecued spareribs

Use a second rack to bake potatoes to go with spareribs. You can also put bread in to heat toward the end of the cooking time.

$^1/_2$ cup honey
$^1/_2$ cup apple juice
2 tablespoons lemon juice
1 small onion, chopped
1 garlic clove, pressed
$^1/_4$ teaspoon Tabasco sauce
1 teaspoon Worcestershire sauce
1 can (8-ounce) tomato sauce
3 pounds pork spareribs
Salt and freshly ground pepper to taste

Combine all ingredients except spareribs and simmer, covered, 15 minutes. Put spareribs on rack over drip tray. Sprinkle with salt and pepper. Bake at floor level for 30 minutes at 350°F. Brush with barbecue sauce and continue baking for 1 hour, brushing with barbecue sauce every 15 minutes. **Makes 4 to 6 servings.**

lamb colcannon

Colcannon is an Irish combination of cabbage, potatoes and onion, made in varying ways depending on which Irish cook one listens to. In this version we bake shoulder lamb chops on top and it makes a fine dinner.

3 cups chopped cooked cabbage
3 cups chopped cooked potatoes
1 large onion, chopped
Leaves from 3 sprigs fresh thyme or $^1/_2$ teaspoon dried
1 teaspoon salt
Freshly ground pepper to taste
1 chicken bouillon cube
$^1/_2$ cup hot water
4 shoulder lamb chops, trimmed of fat

Mix cabbage with potatoes, onion and seasonings. Dissolve chicken bouillon in hot water and mix in lightly. Spoon into a buttered 2-quart casserole large enough in diameter to hold lamb chops on top. Place lamb chops on cabbage-potato mixture. Cover and bake at 350°F for 1 $^1/_2$ hours. **Makes 4 servings.**

meat loaf

Seasonings can be mixed in food processor using the steel blade, then blended with the other ingredients. It makes meat loaf a cinch.

¾ **cup uncooked oatmeal**
1 **medium onion, chopped**
4 **to 5 sprigs parsley, chopped**
1 **teaspoon salt**
¾ **cup water**
1 **egg**
1¼ **pounds ground beef**
½ **pound sweet Italian sausage, casing removed**

Mix oatmeal with onion, seasonings, water and egg in a large bowl. Add beef and sausage and mix lightly until well blended. Put into a 9 ×5 ×4-inch loaf pan and bake at 325°F for 50 to 60 minutes. **Makes 6 to 8 servings.**

Note: This meat loaf is excellent served hot, but it is particularly good for sandwiches when chilled. Cut thin slices and put 2 or 3 in each sandwich.

venison steaks

Heat twice baked potatoes and zucchini squash with the venison steaks.

4 **boneless venison round steaks,**
    about ½ **-pound each, cut at**
    least 1½ **-inches thick**
2 **shallots, chopped**
1 **carrot, sliced**
1 **onion, sliced**
1 **clove garlic, chopped**
2 **or 3 sprigs fresh thyme or**
    ¼ **teaspoon dried**

1 **bay leaf**
1 **or 2 whole cloves, crushed**
2 **or 3 whole peppercorns, crushed**
1 **cup dry white wine**
½ **cup cider vinegar**
2 **tablespoons water**
¼ **cup vegetable oil**
Softened butter or margarine

Put venison steaks into a pan and add remaining ingredients except butter. Cover and marinate in refrigerator overnight or for at least 6 to 8 hours, turning occasionally. When ready to cook remove steaks from marinade and pat dry with paper towels. Remove drip tray and rack from oven and preheat to "BROIL" or 450°F for 10 minutes. Place steaks on rack and spread with softened butter. Broil 15 minutes. If steak is more than 1½-inches thick it can be broiled with the Probe-A-Matic. Insert in steak and set probe dial temperature at 115°F (rare), oven temperature at broil and timer at STAY ON. Generally speaking, game steaks should not be cooked more than medium rare. **Makes 4 servings.**

casa elena stew

A delicious slow cooker recipe which will become one of your favorites. Put it on to cook in the morning and it's ready for guests in the evening. A simple green salad and hot Old Fashioned Sponge Bread are easy to add.

4 slices diced bacon
1 1/2 pounds beef chuck, cubed
1 large garlic clove, crushed
1 large onion, sliced
1/4 teaspoon dried sage
1/4 teaspoon dried marjoram
1 medium bay leaf, cut up
1/2 teaspoon curry powder
1/2 teaspoon paprika
3 medium tomatoes, peeled and diced
2 tablespoons vinegar
3/4 cup water
2 beef bouillon cubes
1/2 cup dry white wine
1/4 cup sliced, stuffed olives
3 sprigs parsley, chopped
4 medium potatoes, peeled

Cook bacon in a 2-quart oven-proof casserole until crisp. Add meat, garlic and onions and cook until meat is lightly browned. Add remaining ingredients. Cover and place on rack in floor position. Set timer at STAY ON and temperature at 225°F. Let cook for 8 to 10 hours. Season to taste with salt and freshly ground pepper. **Makes 4 servings.**

pork ribs and sauerkraut

Have some chilled applesauce and rye bread and butter ready to go with this "one dish slow cooker meal."

3 to 3$^1/_2$ pounds country style pork ribs
1 medium onion, sliced
1 can (1-pound 11-ounce) sauerkraut, rinsed and drained
$^1/_3$ cup brown sugar
3 tablespoons catsup
1 teaspoon salt
$^3/_4$ teaspoon caraway seed
4 potatoes, peeled

Put ribs in bottom of a 3-quart casserole. Add onions, combine sauerkraut with sugar, catsup, salt and caraway seeds and spoon over ribs. Put potatoes on top of sauerkraut. Cover. Cook in oven at 225°F for 8 to 10 hours.
Makes 4 servings.

super corned beef, california style

This marvelously flavored slow-cooked corned beef can be chilled to serve cold for a buffet treat or hot with a choice of vegetables.

1 corned beef brisket (4 to 5 pounds)
2 quarts water
2 cups dry white wine
$^1/_2$ cup finely chopped onion
$^1/_8$ teaspoon garlic powder
1 teaspoon dried dill leaves
2 stalks celery, cut up, include leaves
2 bay leaves
1 small orange, sliced
1 stick cinnamon (about 1$^1/_2$ inch)
3 whole cloves

If necessary, cut corned beef into 2 pieces to fit into a large casserole. Add remaining ingredients and cover tightly. Set timer to STAY ON and temperature to 225°F. Let cook 8 to 10 hours. If corned beef is to be served cold, let cool in cooking liquid. **Makes 10 to 12 servings.**

really hearty slow cooker beef soup

Don't let the long list of ingredients scare you away. This hearty soup is so good you will make it often, using the oven as a slow cooker. With it serve Whole Wheat French Bread, fruit and cheese for dessert and you've a complete meal.

1 leek
1 cup thinly sliced carrots
1 cup thinly sliced celery
1/3 cup barley
1 package (9-ounce) frozen Italian green beans, thawed
1 pound boneless beef chuck, cut in 1/2 -inch cubes
2 teaspoons gravy aid
2 tablespoons all-purpose flour
1 can (16-ounce) undrained whole tomatoes, cut up
1 teaspoon salt
1 teaspoon sugar
1 bay leaf
3 1/2 quarts water
6 beef bouillon cubes
1/4 cup chopped parsley

Wash leek well and put into the bottom of a 3 1/2-quart pan. Add carrots, celery, barley and beans. Mix beef with gravy aid and flour and place on top of vegetables. Add remaining ingredients. Cover and place in oven. Set oven timer at STAY ON and temperature at 225°F. Cook 10 hours. Taste, add more salt if necessary and stir well. **Makes 10 cups or 6 servings.**

Chicken/Fish/Game Birds/ Turkey

Poultry is a natural for the convection oven. The swirling hot air seals in the natural juices, virtually eliminating basting. Roasting time is reduced by 1/3, as well.

When broiling poultry or fish, preheat the oven for 10 minutes with the temperature set at "BROIL" or 450° F. Set the items to be broiled directly on the rack. Remember—no turning is necessary in the convection oven. Delicate fillets can be broiled on a cookie sheet or the drip tray that has been set on the rack.

Plan your menus so that several things can be cooking at one time. Planning saves time and work as well as energy.

roasting chart

VARIETY OF MEAT WITH OVEN TIME		WEIGHT IN POUNDS	APPROX. ROASTING TIME	FROZEN MEATS APPROX. ROASTING TIME	INTERNAL TEMP. AT END OF ROASTING TIME
POULTRY 300°F	Turkey	6-10	1^1/$_2$-2 hrs	3-3^1/$_2$ hrs	180°-185°
	Turkey, stuffed	6-10	1^3/$_4$-2^1/$_2$ hrs		180°-185°
	Turkey	10-14	2-3 hrs	3^1/$_2$-4^1/$_2$ hrs	180°-185°
	Turkey, stuffed	10-14	2^3/$_4$-3^1/$_4$ hrs		180°-185°
	Turkey	14-16+	3-3^1/$_2$ hrs	4-5 hrs	180°-185°
	Turkey, stuffed	14-16+	3^1/$_2$-4 hrs		180°-185°
POULTRY 400°F	Duckling	4-6	1^1/$_2$-1^3/$_4$ hrs		180°-185°
	Duckling, stuffed	4-6	1^3/$_4$-2 hrs		180°-185°
POULTRY 325°F	Roasting Chicken	3^1/$_2$-6	1-1^3/$_4$ hrs	1^3/$_4$-2^1/$_4$ hrs	180°-185°
	Roasting Chicken, stuffed	3^1/$_2$-6	1^1/$_4$-2 hrs		180°185°
	Cornish Game Hens	1-1^1/$_2$	^{3}/$_4$ hr		180°-185°
	Cornish Game Hens, stuffed	1-1^1/$_2$	1 hr		180°-185°

broiling chart

VARIETY OF MEAT WITH OVEN TEMP.	CUT	WEIGHT OR THICKNESS	APPROX. BROILING TIME IN MINUTES*	FROZEN MEATS APPROX. BROILING TIME IN MINUTES
CHICKEN "BROIL" or 450°F	Broiler-Fryer, halved, quartered, or pieces	2-3 lb	30	40
FISH (COD, HADDOCK, FLOUNDER) "BROIL" or 450°F	Fillets Steaks	1/4-1/2 inch 3/4-1 inch	8-10 15-18	15-18 23-26

*Note: Meat should be at refrigerator temperature.

ALL TIMES ARE BASED ON A PREHEATED OVEN.

chicken diego

Put a rice casserole (pg. 59) in oven to bake at same time to serve with chicken.

1 broiler-fryer, cut up or 2 whole chicken breasts
1 cup dry white wine
2 tablespoons chopped fresh parsley or 1 tablespoon dried
2 tablespoons chives
1 teaspoon dried rosemary, crushed
5 tablespoons melted butter or margarine
1/2 cup flour
1 teaspoon salt
Freshly ground pepper to taste
1/2 teaspoon paprika

Cut up chicken, saving boney pieces for soup. If chicken breasts are used, cut into two pieces. Put chicken in a bowl and pour wine over. Cover and refrigerate for 2 to 3 hours. When ready to cook, drain off wine and add to it the parsley, chives, rosemary and butter. Mix together flour, salt, pepper and paprika and coat chicken with mixture. Place chicken pieces in a flat, buttered pan and pour wine mixture over. Cover and bake at 350°F for 30 minutes. Uncover and continue baking 30 minutes longer or until chicken is done. Baste several times during cooking with wine. **Makes 4 servings.**

broiled chicken

The convection oven seals in meat juices so that chicken can be broiled without basting. A simple coating of seasoned salt gives a nice flavor.

1 broiler-fryer, cut in quarters
Seasoned salt to taste

Sprinkle broiler pieces on all sides with seasoned salt. Remove drip tray and rack and preheat oven to "BROIL" or 450°F for 10 minutes. Put chicken on rack and broil for 25 minutes. **Makes 4 servings.**

broiled fish

Put **fish** on buttered drip tray and spread with **softened butter** and sprinkle on a generous amount of **lemon juice**. If you like, add a **dash of paprika**. Thin fillets will take about 5 to 6 minutes and thicker fish steaks 8 to 10 minutes. The oven should be preheated for broil as directed in the broiled chicken recipe.

turkey casserole

The casserole goes in first on the lower position, then 25 minutes later put in the beans and the Corn Raisin Muffins. Some crisp vegetables and fruit for dessert and dinner is ready.

2 tablespoons butter or margarine
4 tablespoons minced onion
1 1/2 tablespoons flour
1 tablespoon chopped parsley
1 tablespoon chopped chives
1/4 teaspoon freshly grated nutmeg
1/2 teaspoon salt
1/2 cup milk
1/4 cup sherry wine
2 egg yolks
2 cups ground cooked turkey
2 egg whites, beaten

Heat butter in saucepan and sauté onion until golden. Add flour, parsley, chives, nutmeg and salt and mix well. Stir in milk and sherry and bring to a boil, stirring constantly. Fold a little of hot mixture into egg yolks and return to sauce, blending well. Add turkey and fold in beaten egg whites. Spoon into a buttered 4-cup casserole and bake at 350°F for about 45 minutes. Serve at once. **Makes 4 servings.**

Green Beans:

Put **1 can (1-pound) drained green beans** (save liquid for soup stock) in a 3-cup casserole and add **2 tablespoons each vinegar, sugar and butter or margarine.** Cover and bake at 350°F for 20 minutes.

Corn Raisin Muffins:

Prepare an **8-ounce package of corn muffin mix** according to package directions, adding **1/2 cup raisins.** Fill 6 2¾-inch muffin tins ⅔ full and bake at 350°F for 20 minutes. **Makes 6 large muffins.**

stuffed peppers

Recently ground raw turkey has been appearing in the meat counter; used in this Stuffed Green Pepper recipe it makes a delicious filling. If you cannot find it, buy the least expensive turkey parts and grind in a food processor or hand grinder.

6 large green peppers
¼ cup butter or margarine
1 cup chopped onion
2 cups ground raw turkey
1¼ cups soft bread crumbs
¼ cup minced parsley
1 teaspoon salt
Freshly ground pepper to taste
2 eggs, beaten

Cut tops off green peppers and remove seeds and white ribs. Heat butter in skillet and cook onion and turkey for 5 minutes, stirring. Add 1 cup crumbs and remaining ingredients mixing lightly to blend. Place peppers upright in a casserole and fill with turkey mixture. Sprinkle remaining crumbs on top. Bake, covered at 375°F for 30 minutes. Uncover and bake 10 minutes longer. **Makes 6 servings.**

turkey loaf

A way to use the ground raw turkey now found in many supermarket meat departments. It is excellent either hot or cold. It makes great sandwiches and is a fine buffet item. Potatoes bake nicely at the same time.

1 cup dry bread crumbs
½ cup apple juice
1 teaspoon salt
Freshly ground pepper to taste
1 stalk celery, chopped
1 medium onion, chopped
1 teaspoon fresh rosemary or ½ teaspoon dried
1 egg
2 pounds ground raw turkey

Combine bread crumbs with remaining ingredients except turkey and blend well. (This is a good job for the food processor, using the steel blade.) Add to the ground turkey and mix until blended. Shape in a greased 9 ×5 ×4-inch loaf pan. Bake at 350°F for 50 to 60 minutes. **Makes 6 to 8 servings.**

homemade chicken pie

Nothing tastes better on a cold night than a homemade chicken pie. Serve with spiced apple rings.

2 cups coarsely cut cooked chicken
1 cup cooked peas
1/2 cup cooked diced carrots
1/2 cup cooked small onions
3 tablespoons chicken fat or butter
4 tablespoons flour
2 cups chicken broth
Salt and freshly ground pepper to taste
Pastry for single crust

Arrange chicken and vegetables in a buttered flat 6-cup pan. Heat chicken fat in saucepan and add flour. Let bubble. Stir in chicken broth and bring to a boil. Season to taste. Pour over chicken and vegetables. Roll pastry into a round about the size of the casserole, and place over chicken and gravy in pan. Trim. Mark into 4ths with a sharp knife. Bake at 375°F for 15 minutes or until pastry is browned and mixture bubbly. **Makes 4 servings.**

dove breasts smetana

Serve Dove Breasts Smetana with Rice in Casserole which can be baked in the oven while the dove is cooking. Broccoli spears and an apple salad can round out the menu. Smetana is the Russian word for sour cream.

18 dove breasts
1 medium onion, chopped
2 tablespoons butter or margarine
1 can (10½-ounce) cream of celery soup
1 can (3-ounce) sliced mushrooms
½ cup dry white wine
¼ teaspoon oregano
¼ teaspoon rosemary
Freshly ground pepper to taste
1 cup dairy sour cream
Paprika

Place breasts in a large buttered casserole so they are not crowded. Sauté onion in butter until tender. Add remaining ingredients except sour cream and paprika and stir to blend. Pour over breasts. Cover casserole and bake at 325°F for 60 minutes. Turn birds several times during cooking. At the end of this time gently stir in sour cream, sprinkle with paprika and continue baking, uncovered, for 20 minutes. Planning 3 breasts per serving. **Makes 6 servings.**

Rice In Casserole:

Put **1 cup rice** in a buttered 5-cup casserole. Add **2 cups water**, ¼ **cup chopped parsley**, ½ **teaspoon salt** and **3 tablespoons soft butter or margarine**. Cover and bake at 325°F while the doves are cooking. Stir rice before serving. **Makes 6 servings.**

broiled wild duck

Serve Casserole of Noodles and Cottage Cheese with the ducks, tiny peas and romaine salad. Hot crisp Italian bread would be good, too.

4 wild ducks
1 clove garlic
$1/2$ cup soy sauce
$1/2$ cup bourbon whiskey
$1/2$ cup oil
$1/2$ teaspoon grated ginger

Split ducks and remove backbone. Combine remaining ingredients and marinate ducks overnight in the refrigerator. Turn ducks in marinade occasionally. When ready to cook, remove drip tray and rack from oven and put second rack in third position. Preheat on "BROIL" or 450°F for 10 minutes. Place ducks on rack and broil 16 to 18 minutes. **This will serve 4,** depending on appetites and size of ducks.

Casserole Of Noodles And Cottage Cheese:

Cook **8 ounces of noodles** as directed on package. Drain and mix with **1 cup smooth cottage cheese, 1 teaspoon chopped fresh basil** or **$1/2$ teaspoon dried** and season to taste with **salt** and **pepper.** Spoon into a buttered flat casserole. Sprinkle **buttered crumbs** on top and bake on second rack while ducks are broiling, about 10 to 15 minutes.

Crisp Italian Bread:

Cut **Italian bread** in thick chunks and **butter.** Place on rack with noodles 5 minutes before the ducks are done.

lobster quiche

This makes a show piece at a buffet meal, as it well should.

1 9-inch unbaked pie shell
1 can (5-ounce) lobster or crab meat
¹/₂ cup grated Swiss cheese
¹/₄ cup grated sharp Cheddar cheese
¹/₄ cup grated Parmesan cheese
4 eggs, beaten
2 cups half-and-half
¹/₂ teaspoon salt
Freshly ground pepper to taste
Freshly ground nutmeg

Prick bottom of pie shell and bake at 300°F for 15 to 20 minutes or until light brown. Dice lobster. Spread in bottom of pastry shell. Sprinkle with cheeses. Combine remaining ingredients except nutmeg and pour over lobster and cheese. Sprinkle with nutmeg. Bake at 300°F for 40 minutes or until knife inserted near center comes out clean. Let stand 10 minutes before cutting. Serve warm or cold. **Makes 4 servings.**

shrimp casserole

Tomato halves sprinkled with seasoned salt can be baked along with the casserole. Put the tomatoes and some French bread in with the casserole the last 15 minutes of cooking.

¾ **cup chopped onion**
1 **cup chopped celery**
3 **tablespoons butter or margarine**
1½ **cups uncooked long grain rice**
1 **can (4½ ounces) tiny shrimp, undrained**
¼ **cup dry white wine**
4 **tablespoons chopped parsley**
4 **cups boiling water**
½ **teaspoon salt**
¼ **teaspoon black pepper**
¼ **teaspoon garlic powder**
American cheese slices (optional)

Sauté onion and celery in butter until tender, but not brown. Add rice, shrimp, wine and parsley. Continue stirring over low heat for 2 minutes. Pour rice mixture into greased 2-quart casserole. Dissolve bouillon cubes in boiling water. Pour over rice mixture. Stir in remaining ingredients. Cover casserole and bake at 350°F for 50 to 60 minutes or until rice is cooked. Fluff rice with fork and serve. If desired, after fluffing rice, place slices of American cheese on casserole and place in oven 5 to 10 minutes, or until cheese melts. Serve immediately. **Makes 6 servings**.

salmon mushroom loaf

Salmon Mushroom Loaf and Rice Casserole make a nice base for an oven dinner. Steam green beans and serve crisp lettuce hearts with it. A food processor makes preparation a snap.

³/₄ cup chopped fresh mushrooms
4 tablespoons finely chopped onions
2 tablespoons butter or margarine
1 egg
¹/₂ cup dry white wine
1 cup fresh white bread crumbs
¹/₂ teaspoon salt
Freshly ground pepper to taste
2 tablespoons lemon juice
1 can (15¹/₂ or 16-ounce) pink or red salmon

Cook mushrooms and onions in butter for about 5 minutes, stirring. Beat egg with wine, add cooked vegetables, bread crumbs, salt, pepper and lemon juice and mix well. Drain and flake salmon and remove bones. Stir into crumb mixture. Spoon into a greased 8 ×4 ×2¹/₄-inch loaf pan. Bake at 350°F for 40 to 50 minutes until knife inserted in center comes out clean. Let stand in pan 5 minutes. Slice and serve. **Makes 4 servings.**

Rice In Casserole:

Put ³/₄ **cup natural rice** in a buttered 1 quart casserole. Add 1¹/₂ **cups water,** ¹/₂ **teaspoon salt,** ¹/₄ **cup chopped celery,** ¹/₄ **cup chopped parsley** and **3 tablespoons soft butter or margarine.** Stir. If necessary, add a little additional **water** during cooking. Cover and bake in oven (350°F for 1 hour) with Salmon Mushroom Loaf. Stir rice before serving. **Makes 4 servings.**

fish with mushrooms

Very fine buttered noodles and steamed broccoli would complement the fish nicely. Heat garlic bread in foil while the fish is baking.

2 tablespoons chopped onion
2 tablespoons chopped parsley
1½ pounds white fish fillets
½ pound fresh mushrooms
4 tablespoons butter or margarine
½ cup dry white wine
Salt and freshly ground pepper to taste

Butter generously a flat baking dish and sprinkle onion and parsley on bottom. Arrange fish in 4 serving portions on top of onion. Chop mushroom stems and tops and sauté in butter until dry. Spread over fish and pour wine over all. Season to taste with salt and pepper. Bake at 375°F for 15 to 20 minutes or until fish flakes easily with fork. Serve fish with mushrooms and sauce in pan. **Makes 4 servings.**

snappy perch fillets

A delicious way to season fish. Serve with French fried potatoes heated in the oven at the same time and a wedge of lettuce with russian dressing.

1 pound frozen ocean perch fillets
3 tablespoons Worcestershire sauce
3 tablespoons lemon juice
2 tablespoons chili sauce
2 tablespoons steak sauce
1 teaspoon grated horseradish
1 tablespoon prepared mustard
¾ cup dried bread crumbs
2 tablespoons melted butter or margarine

Defrost perch fillets and separate. Place skin side down in a buttered flat baking dish. Mix seasonings and spoon over fillets. (There will be some left over to serve with cooked fish.) Let stand 30 minutes. Mix crumbs and butter. Set aside. Bake at 400°F for 15 minutes. Sprinkle with crumbs and bake 5 minutes longer. Serve any leftover sauce. **Makes 2 to 3 servings.**

baked stuffed fish

Baked stuffed fish is a good looking and good tasting way to serve a whole fish. Heat Parsleyed Potatoes to go with fish.

3 green onions, thinly sliced
3 mushrooms, chopped
2 tablespoons butter or margarine
$1/2$ cup dry bread crumbs
$1/4$ cup chopped parsley
2 or 3 sprigs fresh thyme or $1/2$ teaspoon dried
$1/2$ teaspoon salt
1 tablespoon lemon juice
*1 (3- to 4-pound) whole fish
Softened butter or margarine

Sauté onions and mushrooms in butter until tender. Stir in crumbs, parsley, seasonings and lemon juice. Cool slightly. Fish may be baked with or without head—your preference. Cut out large fins and gills. Wash well inside and out. Butter drip tray generously with softened butter. Place fish on drip tray and fill with stuffing. If the stuffing has a tendency to fall out, fasten edges of fish together with wooden picks. Rub fish with butter. Bake in center position at 350°F for 30 minutes or until fish flakes easily with a fork. **Makes 4 servings.**

---

*If you do not have a whole fish, bake the stuffing between 2 fillets weighing about $1 1/2$ pounds each.

Parsleyed Potatoes:

Drain a **1-pound can of potatoes** and put into a flat metal baking dish. Dot with **butter or margarine** and add **salt** and **freshly ground pepper** to taste. Bake at 350°F with the fish, turning potatoes in pan several times. To serve, sprinkle with **chopped parsley. Makes 4 servings.**

baked spanish mackerel

Buttered macaroni, creamed spinach and a salad of chopped celery and apple could complete the menu.

**4 cleaned mackerel, about 1
    pound each
1 fresh lemon**

**Salt
Freshly ground pepper
Softened butter**

Wash mackerel and place in an oiled baking pan. Squeeze fresh lemon juice over the fish. Season to taste with salt and pepper. Spread with softened butter. Bake at 400°F for 15 minutes or until fish flakes easily with a fork. Serve with additional fresh lemon wedges. **Makes 4 servings.**

herbed roast chicken

Serve Herbed Roast Chicken and Onion Roasted Potatoes with a green vegetable and cranberry sauce.

**5 pound (about) roasting chicken
Several sprigs fresh or dried thyme, sage, parsley
Small onion, halved
Salt
Freshly ground pepper
Softened butter or margarine**

Wash and dry roaster. Put herbs and onion in cavity. Rub skin with salt, pepper and butter. Put chicken directly on rack and put rack, chicken and drip tray in floor position. Insert probe connection into right side of oven. Insert probe in chicken, between breast and thigh, being sure it does not touch bone. Set probe temperature dial between 180° and 185°F. Set oven temperature to 325°F and timer to STAY ON*. Remove chicken from oven and let stand 10 to 15 minutes before carving. Skim fat from pan juices in drip tray and serve pan juices with chicken if desired.

*****Note:** If your convection oven does not have a Probe-A-Matic Control, set temperature at 325°F, timer at 1 1/2 hours, allowing about 18 minutes per pound or 180° to 185°F on meat thermometer.

Onion Roasted Potatoes:

Peel **4 baking potatoes** and slice crosswise into thirds, but do not cut completely through. Put **thin onion slices** between potato slices. Place potatoes in squares of heavy aluminum foil and brush generously with **melted butter.** Sprinkle each potato with about **1 teaspoon dry onion soup mix.** Fold foil around potatoes and seal. Put into oven at same time as chicken. **Makes 4 servings.**

chicken casserole

Heat butterfly rolls while the casserole is cooking. Add some pineapple slices to plate when serving the chicken.

2 cups diced cooked chicken
2 cups thinly sliced celery
1 can (1-pound 1-ounce) whole kernel corn, drained
³/₄ cup mayonnaise
¹/₃ cup toasted, slivered almonds
2 tablespoons lemon juice
2 teaspoons grated onion
Salt and freshly ground pepper to taste
¹/₂ cup shredded American cheese
1 cup crushed potato chips

Lightly mix chicken with all ingredients except cheese and chips. Spoon into a buttered 2-quart casserole. Sprinkle with cheese and top with chips. Bake at 400°F for 15 to 20 minutes. **Makes 8 servings.**

duckling cooked in wine

A duckling cooked in wine calls for rice or noodles as an accompaniment. Steamed carrots and onions could be the vegetable and greens with grapefruit sections the salad.

1 duckling (4 to 5 pounds)
1 large onion, sliced
1 sprig parsley
2 bay leaves
1 teaspoon salt
2 cups dry red wine
Freshly ground pepper to taste
¹/₄ cup brandy
1 tablespoon oil
¹/₂ pound fresh mushrooms, sliced

Cut duck into quarters and put into a large casserole. Add remaining ingredients except oil and mushrooms. Cover and marinate in refrigerator 4 to 5 hours or overnight, turning occasionally. When ready to cook, remove duck from marinade and pat dry. Heat oil in skillet and brown duck on all sides. Return to marinade, add mushrooms and bake duck at 325°F for 1¹/₂ hours or until duck is tender. Strain the sauce and remove grease. Serve some with the duck. **Makes 4 servings.**

roast pheasant

Rice with mushrooms and braised celery would be elegant with the pheasant.

3 dressed pheasants
¼ cup butter or margarine
8 shallots
½ cup brandy
3 slices bacon
2 cups chicken stock
1 pint heavy cream
Salt and freshly ground pepper to taste

Truss pheasants so they will not lose shape and brown in butter with shallots on all sides. When pheasants are browned, pour brandy over and blaze. Cover pheasant breasts with bacon and place pheasants in a baking dish. Add chicken stock to skillet and cook and stir to remove crust from skillet. Pour over pheasants in pan and roast, uncovered, at 375°F for 30 minutes basting several times. Add cream to sauce and roast 15 minutes longer, basting several times. Remove pheasants to platter and season sauce to taste with salt and pepper. Serve pheasants with sauce and currant jelly.
Makes 6 to 8 servings.

Vegetables

Vegetables can partner easily with main dishes. Slip them into the oven while roasting or broiling and your whole meal can be done at once. A great way to save time and energy.

Canned or frozen vegetables are heated quickly in the convection oven. The addition of chopped celery, onions, pimientos, herbs or spices can perk up otherwise hum-drum vegetables.

Fresh vegetables can be baked or broiled. Leave them plain or spark them up with spices, butter or cheese.

baked squash casserole

This tasty squash casserole would be good with chicken, pork or beef. Bake this casserole while meat is roasting.

2 cups mashed cooked butternut (or other) squash
$^1/_2$ teaspoon salt
3 tablespoons brown sugar
3 tablespoons butter or margarine
4 tablespoons tawny port
$^1/_2$ teaspoon cinnamon

Combine all ingredients and mix well. Spoon into a buttered flat casserole and bake at 300°F for about 30 minutes or until hot through. **Makes 4 servings.**

acorn squash piquant

Acorn squash is a wonderful vegetable. It particularly complements ham and pork. Baked pork chops can be done the same time as this recipe for squash.

2 medium-sized acorn squash
4 tablespoons softened butter or margarine
$\frac{1}{2}$ teaspoon freshly ground nutmeg
4 tablespoons brown sugar
2 tablespoons frozen orange juice concentrate

Wash and cut squash in half lengthwise and remove seeds. Spread cut surface with butter and sprinkle with nutmeg. Place in a pan, cut side up, and pour water in pan to 1 inch deep. Position on center shelf. Bake at 350°F for about 30 minutes. Mix brown sugar with orange juice concentrate. Spread on cut surface of baked squash and continue baking about 15 minutes or until squash is tender and browned. **Makes 4 servings.**

Baked Pork Chops:

Mix $\frac{1}{4}$ **cup flour,** $\frac{1}{2}$ **cup dry bread crumbs,** $\frac{1}{2}$ **teaspoon** each **paprika, garlic** and **celery salt, 1 teaspoon Beau Monde seasoning, freshly ground pepper** to taste. Dip **4 pork chops** cut $\frac{3}{4}$-inch thick in **milk** and then in **flour mixture.** Place on greased rack over drip tray in floor position and bake at 350°F for 45 minutes. **Makes 4 servings.**

sweet potato-apple casserole

A delightful fall vegetable casserole. Bake Sausage Patties at same time to make an oven menu.

4 medium sweet potatoes
4 medium cooking apples
$\frac{1}{2}$ cup firmly packed brown sugar
$\frac{1}{2}$ teaspoon salt
$\frac{1}{2}$ teaspoon cinnamon
4 tablespoons butter or margarine
1 tablespoon lemon juice
$\frac{1}{2}$ cup apple juice

Cook potatoes until just tender. Cool, peel and cut into 1-inch thick slices. Peel and core apples and slice into $\frac{1}{2}$ inch rings. Mix sugar, salt and cinnamon. Arrange potato slices and apples in alternate layers in a buttered 2-quart casserole, sprinkling some of the sugar mixture on each layer. Dot top with butter. Mix lemon juice with apple juice and pour over casserole. Cover and bake at 350°F for 30 minutes. Uncover and bake 10 minutes longer. **Makes 6 servings.**

Sausage Patties:

Combine **1$\frac{1}{2}$ pounds bulk sausage** with **1 cup dry bread crumbs**, **$\frac{1}{2}$ cup tomato juice** and **1 egg**. Shape into 6 patties and place in a shallow baking dish. Top each patty with a slice of onion. Bake at 350°F for 40 minutes. **Makes 6 servings.**

twice baked sweet potatoes

The potatoes can be prepared in advance and refrigerated until ready to reheat. Add about 5 minutes to reheating time if this is done.

6 medium sweet potatoes
4 tablespoons butter or margarine
2 tablespoons maple syrup
1/2 teaspoon salt
1/2 cup cornflake crumbs (about)

Scrub potatoes and bake at 375°F for 45 to 50 minutes or until tender. When cool enough to handle, cut strip off top of each potato and scoop out insides into a bowl, being careful not to break skin. Whip potatoes with butter, maple syrup and salt until light and fluffy. If more liquid is needed, add a little milk. Lightly pile whipped potatoes back into shells and sprinkle tops with cornflake crumbs. To reheat, bake at 375°F for 10 to 12 minutes. **Makes 6 servings.**

swedish potatoes

These are good potatoes to cook with a roast—which is why the 300°F temperature is used. They can also be baked at 325°F or 400°F, with a reduction in length of cooking time.

Any number of **potatoes** to suit the diners. Peel baking potatoes and slice down in thin slices almost to bottom. A tip from a Swedish friend—put the handle of a wooden spoon on the far side of the potato and cut down to the spoon in making the slices—you can never go too far and slice through the potato. Spread with **melted butter** and sprinkle with **garlic salt** and **paprika** and roast at 300°F for about 1 ½ hours, depending on size of potatoes. Brush with butter several times during cooking.

scalloped potatoes

A recipe that can be multiplied up or divided down, to go into the oven with meatloaf or some other main dish.

2 large potatoes
2 tablespoons flour
4 tablespoons butter or margarine
Salt and freshly ground pepper to taste
1 cup hot milk
4 tablespoons dry bread crumbs

Peel potatoes and slice thin. Layer in a flat buttered baking dish with some of flour, butter, salt and pepper over each layer. Pour milk over all and sprinkle with dry bread crumbs. Bake at 300°F for about 45 minutes or until potatoes are tender when pierced with a fork. **Makes 4 servings.**

twice baked potatoes

The potatoes may be prepared in advance and heated toward the end of the cooking time for a roast or casserole.

4 baking potatoes
6 tablespoons milk (about)
4 tablespoons butter
2 tablespoons chopped chives
1/2 teaspoon paprika
Salt and freshly ground pepper to taste

Scrub baking potatoes. If desired, potatoes may be rubbed with oil. Bake at 400°F for 45 minutes or until potatoes are soft when pressed with fingers. Remove from oven and cool enough to handle. Cut enough off tops to scoop out inside of potatoes into a bowl, being careful not to break skin. Mash potatoes with remaining ingredients and beat until light and fluffy, adding more milk, if necessary. Season to taste with salt and pepper. Pile mashed potatoes lightly back into shells. Sprinkle with paprika. Reheat at 400°F for 15 minutes or until potatoes are lightly browned and hot. **Makes 4 servings.**

oven steamed pumpkin

In the fall when pumpkins are plentiful, oven steam to use at once or store in the freezer. Pumpkin can be used to make cookies (page 101), pumpkin pie or custard or serve as a vegetable with the addition of brown sugar and butter.

Depending on the size of the **pumpkin**, cut into manageable pieces and remove seeds. Wash well. Put in a large, flat pan, cut side down with a small amount of **water** in the bottom of the pan. Bake at 300°F for 30 minutes or until pumpkin is tender when pierced with a fork. Cool enough to handle and scoop out and mash pumpkin. To freeze, pack into containers, leaving a 1-inch head space. Cover, label and date. Freeze. Pumpkin will keep 12 months. Pumpkin stored, covered, in the refrigerator will keep about 10 days.

grilled pepper salad

Serve this salad with your summer cold plates. It is tasty and pretty.

6 large green peppers
1 clove garlic, crushed
¼ teaspoon salt
2 tablespoons wine vinegar
6 tablespoons olive oil

Preheat oven to "BROIL" or 450°F for 10 minutes. Broil peppers until skins start to brown and blister on all sides, about 10 minutes. Wrap peppers in a clean dish towel and set aside 5 minutes. Remove skins under running water. Cut out stem ends and remove seeds. Cut peppers lengthwise into 1-inch strips. Combine remaining ingredients and pour over pepper strips, turning to coat all peppers. Cover and chill 6 to 8 hours. Serve with a cold plate or on lettuce. **Makes 6 servings.**

sour cream onion squares

Serve these Onion Squares in place of potatoes. They could go in the oven 20 minutes or so before a meat loaf is done.

2 cups sliced Spanish onions
2 tablespoons butter or margarine
¼ teaspoon salt
Freshly ground pepper to taste
½ cup dairy sour cream
1 egg, beaten
½ teaspoon dried dill
2 tablespoons chopped parsley
2 cups buttermilk biscuit mix
⅔ cup milk

Sauté onions in butter until golden. Season with salt and pepper. Reserve. Mix sour cream with egg, dill and parsley. Lightly combine biscuit mix and milk and spread on bottom of a greased 9-inch square baking pan. Spread cooked onions on top. Spoon sour cream mixture over onions. Bake at 325°F for 20 minutes or until topping is set and starting to brown. Cut in squares and serve warm. **Makes about 16 squares.**

easy scalloped cabbage

Easy Scalloped Cabbage would pair well with roast pork. Spiced apple-ring salad could also be a tasty addition to the meal.

1 medium head cabbage, coarsely shredded
1 can (10½-ounce) condensed cream of mushroom soup
¼ cup milk
2 tablespoons butter or margarine
Salt and freshly ground pepper to taste
½ cup buttered bread crumbs

Cook cabbage in boiling water until tender, about 7 minutes. Combine soup with milk and butter and heat. Mix with drained, cooked cabbage and season to taste. Spoon into a buttered 1½-quart casserole. Sprinkle with crumbs and bake at 350°F about 15 minutes or until heated through. **Makes 6 servings.**

sweet and sour cabbage

This recipe, of German origin, is terrific along with pork and baked sweet potatoes.

1 medium head red cabbage (about 3 pounds)
2 cooking apples
¼ cup butter or margarine
½ teaspoon nutmeg
2 tablespoons cider vinegar
2 tablespoons brown sugar
½ cup raisins
Salt and freshly ground pepper to taste

Shred cabbage finely. Peel, core and chop apples. Combine cabbage, apples and remaining ingredients in casserole. Bake at 400°F for 1 hour, stirring occasionally. **Makes 4 to 6 servings.**

lentils en casserole

Serve these lentils and mushrooms as an accompaniment to lamb. A green salad with tomato wedges and Syrian bread would also be good additions.

1 cup dried lentils
3 cups water
1 cup chopped onion
¼ pound sliced fresh mushrooms
3 tablespoons vegetable oil
Salt and freshly ground pepper to taste

Wash lentils and cook in water on low heat for about 40 minutes or until tender. Most of the liquid should be absorbed. Sauté onion and mushrooms in oil for 5 minutes. Combine with lentils, add salt and pepper to taste. Spoon into a buttered 1½-quart casserole. Cover and bake at 350°F for 20 minutes. **Makes 4 servings.**

tangy oven beets

The spicy beets can bake with a meat loaf to become part of an oven meal which includes baked potatoes and a salad of cottage cheese and chopped celery.

4 cups sliced cooked beets*
3 tablespoons butter or margarine
1 tablespoon flour
2 tablespoons brown sugar
3 tablespoons vinegar
¼ cup water
¼ teaspoon cinnamon
Dash each ground nutmeg, ground
**   cloves**
½ teaspoon salt

Put beets into a buttered 1½-quart casserole. Melt butter and stir in flour, then add remaining ingredients and cook and stir until thickened. Pour over beets. Bake, covered, at 350°F for 20 minutes. **Makes 6 servings.**

---

*If canned beets are used, drain well.

ratatouille

The baked ratatouille may also be served cold. Either hot or cold, sliced hard cooked eggs and crusty rye bread would be fine accompaniments.

2 cloves garlic, chopped
1 onion, sliced
1 green pepper, seeded and cut in strips
¼ cup olive oil
3 tomatoes, peeled, chopped
1 medium eggplant, peeled and cubed
4 teaspoons chopped fresh basil or 2 teaspoons dried
2 teaspoons fresh oregano or 1 teaspoon dried
1½ teaspoons salt
Freshly ground pepper to taste
¼ cup chopped fresh parsley
3 medium zucchini, cut in ¼-inch slices

Sauté garlic, onion and green pepper in olive oil in a 3-quart oven-proof saucepan until tender but not browned. Add tomatoes and simmer for 5 minutes. Add remaining ingredients and bring just to a boil. Spoon into a buttered 2-quart casserole. Cover and bake at 350°F for 20 to 25 minutes or until vegetables are tender. Serve hot or chilled. **Makes 6 servings.**

corn pudding

Corn pudding can be served with oven cooked bacon and celery slaw.

4 eggs, slightly beaten
1 can (17 ounces) whole kernel corn, drained
2 tablespoons finely chopped green pepper
2 tablespoons grated onion
1 teaspoon sugar
1/2 teaspoon salt
Freshly ground pepper to taste
1 3/4 cups milk
2 tablespoons butter or margarine

Combine eggs with corn, vegetables and seasonings. Scald milk. Stir in butter until melted. Add gradually to vegetable mixture. Stir to combine. Pour into a buttered 1 1/2-quart casserole and bake at 300°F for about 50 minutes or until a knife inserted in center comes out clean. **Makes 4 to 6 servings.**

escalloped corn and tomatoes

A basic recipe to which you can add seasonings of herbs to suit your fancy. And a wonderful way to use fresh vegetables.

2 1/2 cups corn cut off the cob
3 medium ripe tomatoes, sliced
1/2 green pepper, chopped
1 medium onion, grated
1 teaspoon salt
Freshly ground pepper to taste
1/2 cup buttered bread crumbs

Layer corn, tomatoes, green pepper and onion in a buttered 5-cup casserole. Sprinkle layers with salt and pepper. Top with buttered crumbs. Bake at 350°F for 45 minutes or until hot and bubbly. **Makes 4 to 6 servings.**

Bread/Muffins/Rolls

There is nothing more tantalizing than the smell of freshly baked bread or rolls. Your convection oven makes baking in your own home easier than ever.

Professional bakeries have used convection ovens for years to turn out picture perfect breads. You can do the same. Use your convection oven to let the bread proof (rise). Set the temperature dial to the left edge of the 150°F setting or between the end of the black line and the 150°F setting. Air should feel warm not hot. Place the dough in a greased bowl and cover tightly. Set in the oven. Let proof (rise) according to recipe directions.

Your family's favorites can be adapted to the convection oven. When using a recipe containing leavening (yeast, baking powder, baking soda, etc.) reduce the oven temperature by 75° but not lower than 300°F. Bake as usual—that's all there is to it!

sweet pizza

Sweet Pizza can be served at breakfast, with midmorning coffee or as a dessert with a little jam.

2¼ cups all-purpose flour
1 envelope active dry yeast
3 tablespoons sugar
½ teaspoon salt
¼ cup melted butter or margarine
⅓ cup milk
3 tablespoons sweet sherry
1 egg
Grated rind of one lemon
1 egg yolk
Pared, sliced fruits*
2 tablespoons sugar
¼ teaspoon cinnamon

Mix 1 cup flour with yeast, 3 tablespoons sugar and salt in a bowl. Heat butter, milk and sherry together until bubbles just begin to form. Pour into flour mixture and beat vigorously until smooth. Add egg, 1 cup flour and lemon rind and beat until blended. Put remaining flour on a smooth surface and knead dough for 5 minutes. Put in an oiled bowl, turn dough to oil top and cover tightly. Let rise in oven with temperature set to the the left edge of the 150°F setting or between the end of the black line and the 150° setting. Air should feel warm not hot. Let proof until double in bulk, about 1 hour. Roll or pat dough to fit into a greased 13 ×9 ×2-inch pan. Brush top with beaten egg yolk and let rise again, without covering, as above until double in bulk. Press fruit lightly into top of dough. Mix together remaining sugar and cinnamon and sprinkle over fruit. Bake at 325°F for 20 to 25 minutes or until nicely browned. Cut in squares to serve.

---

*Suggested fruits include any one or combination of apples, peaches, apricots and plums.

breakfast log

This recipe makes two Breakfast Logs—one for now, one for later—or a welcome gift to a friend.

3/4 **cup uncooked oatmeal**
1/4 **cup chopped walnuts**
1/4 **cup chopped dates**
1/4 **cup chopped candied fruits**
1 cup milk
1/4 **cup butter or margarine**
1/4 **cup brown sugar**
1 teaspoon salt
3 cups all-purpose flour (about)
1 package active dry yeast
1 egg
Softened butter or margarine
1/4 **cup granulated sugar**
1 teaspoon cinnamon

Mix together oatmeal, chopped nuts and fruits and set aside. Combine milk, butter, brown sugar and salt and heat until bubbles begin to form around edge of milk. Butter does not need to be completely melted. Beat in 2 cups flour, yeast and egg and continue beating 2 minutes. Stir in oatmeal mixture and enough additional flour to make a soft dough. Turn onto a lightly floured board and knead until elastic, about 10 minutes. Put into a greased bowl and turn to grease dough. Cover tightly. Let rise in oven with temperature set to the left edge of the 150°F setting or between the end of the black line and the 150°F setting. Air should feel warm, not hot. Let proof until double in bulk. About 45 minutes. Punch down and let rest 10 minutes. Divide dough into 2 equal parts. Roll or pat into rectangles 10 ×7 inches. Spread with softened butter and sprinkle with mixed sugar and cinnamon. Roll each from long side and pinch edges to seal. Place on a greased 15 ×10-inch pan. With a scissors make cuts 1 inch apart, almost to bottom. Turn slices on side. Brush with softened butter. Let rise, with oven set as above until doubled in bulk, about 30 minutes. Bake at 300°F for 20 to 25 minutes. While hot, spread with frosting made by mixing **1 cup confectioners' sugar** with **4 teaspoons hot water**. If you wish to freeze one coffee cake, do not frost it until thawed and ready to use. These freeze well, will keep 3 to 4 weeks in 0° freezer.

double corn bread

This is a cross between spoon bread and corn bread. Serve it hot with browned sausages and fried apple slices for a light supper or brunch. Fresh corn is available in the markets almost all year now.

$^3/_4$ **cup yellow cornmeal**
2 teaspoons baking powder
1 tablespoon sugar
$^1/_2$ **cup all-purpose flour**
$^1/_2$ **teaspoon salt**
2 eggs, beaten
1$^1/_2$ cups milk
1 cup corn cut off the cob
$^1/_4$ **cup melted butter**

Mix cornmeal with baking powder, sugar, flour and salt in a bowl. Mix together remaining ingredients and add to dry ingredients, stirring just to moisten. Pour into a buttered 6-cup casserole and bake at 300°F for about 40 minutes or until bread is set. Serve hot with lots of butter. **Makes 6 servings.**

cheer-up muffins

Muffins seem to fit into any meal. These with a peanut butter flavor would be particularly good at breakfast or with a hearty soup for lunch.

$^2/_3$ **cup brown sugar, firmly packed**
$^1/_3$ **cup peanut butter**
1 egg
1 cup milk
1 cup uncooked quick-cooking oatmeal
1 cup all-purpose flour
$^1/_2$ **cup wheat germ**
3 teaspoons baking powder
$^1/_2$ **teaspoon salt**
$^1/_2$ **teaspoon cinnamon**

Beat together sugar, peanut butter and egg until well blended. Gradually stir in milk. Mix oatmeal with flour, wheat germ, baking powder, salt and cinnamon and add to sugar mixture, stirring just until dry ingredients are moistened. Fill 12 paper lined 2 to 2$^1/_2$ -inch muffin pans $^2/_3$ full. Bake at 325°F for 18 to 20 minutes or until wooden pick inserted in center comes out clean. Serve warm. **Makes 1 dozen muffins.** To reheat muffins, wrap in aluminum foil and reheat at 325°F for about 10 minutes.

hot cross buns

Hot Cross Buns were served in England in the pre-Christian era to honor the Goddess of Spring. Today they are made especially at Lent. The buns are good enough to make any time of year, and the frosting does not have to be in the form of a cross.

1 package active dry yeast
$\frac{1}{2}$ cup warm water
$\frac{1}{4}$ cup sugar
$\frac{1}{2}$ teaspoon salt
$\frac{1}{2}$ teaspoon cinnamon
2 tablespoons softened butter or margarine
1 egg
$2\frac{1}{2}$ cups (about) all-purpose flour
$\frac{1}{2}$ cup raisins
1 egg yolk, beaten
1 cup sifted confectioners' sugar
1 tablespoon (about) hot water

Soften yeast in warm water in a medium-sized bowl. Add sugar, salt, cinnamon, butter, egg and 1 cup flour. Beat vigorously. Stir in enough additional flour to make a soft dough. Add raisins and knead on floured board for 5 minutes or until dough is smooth. Cut dough into 12 pieces and shape into round balls. Place in a well greased 8 ×8 ×2-inch pan. Spread top of dough with beaten egg yolk. Set temperature to the left edge of the 150°F setting or between the end of the black line and the 150°F setting. Air should feel warm, not hot. Set timer for 1 hour and let rise until doubled in bulk. Bake at 350°F for 30 minutes. Loosen rolls from sides of pan and turn out on rack. Cool 10 to 15 minutes. Mix confectioners' sugar with enough water to be able to drizzle mixture from a spoon across tops of buns to make a cross on each one. **Makes 1 dozen.**

brioche

Brioche is perfect for a brunch. Since the dough is refrigerated overnight, it can be shaped and baked in time to serve hot from the oven. This is a simplified version of the French brioche, but oh, so good.

¼ **cup milk**
1 **cup butter or margarine**
½ **cup sugar**
1 **teaspoon salt**
4½ **cups (about) all-purpose flour**
2 **packages active dry yeast**
6 **eggs, beaten**
1 **egg yolk**
2 **teaspoons water**

Heat milk, butter, sugar and salt together until butter is melted. Cool slightly and beat in 1 cup flour and yeast. Add 2 more cups flour and eggs and beat with electric mixer for about 5 minutes. Add remaining 1½ cups flour and beat until mixture is smooth. Cover tightly and let rise in oven with temperature set to the left edge of the 150°F setting or between the end of the black line and the 150°F setting. Air should feel warm, not hot. Let rise for about 45 minutes or until doubled in bulk. Stir batter down. Keep tightly covered and refrigerate overnight. When ready to bake, grease well 1 dozen 2-inch muffin pans. Grease hands and shape two-thirds of the dough into 1 dozen balls about half the size of the muffin pan and place in greased pans. Shape remaining dough into 1 dozen small balls. Press into larger dough balls in muffin pans. Brush with oil. Let rise until doubled in bulk with oven set as above, about 35 minutes. Preheat oven to 325°F and bake for 15 minutes or until nicely browned. About 5 minutes before brioche is finished baking, mix egg yolk with water and brush tops to give a nice glaze. Let stand in pan on rack about 5 minutes before removing from pan. **Makes 1 dozen large brioche.**

Note: For a smaller size, make 1½ or 2 dozen in smaller muffin pans.

whole wheat french bread

This whole wheat French bread freezes well—use one loaf from the oven and freeze the other.

1 package active dry yeast
1 1/2 cups warm water
1 tablespoon sugar
1 teaspoon salt
2 tablespoons butter or margarine
3 cups whole wheat flour
1 cup all-purpose white flour
Cornmeal

Combine yeast, water, sugar, salt and butter. Mix well and let stand 5 minutes. Gradually add whole wheat flour, beating well. Add white flour until a dough stiff enough to knead is formed. Knead on a lightly floured board for 8 to 10 minutes or until dough is smooth and elastic. Put into a greased bowl and turn to grease dough. Cover tightly. Set oven temperature to the left edge of the 150°F setting or between the end of the black line and the 150°F setting. Air should feel warm, not hot. Let rise until double in bulk, about 1 hour. Remove dough from oven. Punch down and let rest 10 minutes. Divide into 2 parts and shape into 2 long loaves. Place on a baking sheet that has been sprinkled lightly with cornmeal. Let rise in oven for 10 minutes. Place an 8-inch baking pan half filled with water on floor of oven. Set rack in center of oven. Preheat oven to 350°F for 10 minutes. Cut diagonal gashes across bread loaves and brush tops with water. Bake about 25 to 30 minutes until browned and crusty.
Makes 2 loaves.

old-fashioned sponge bread

The convection oven is perfect for Old-Fashioned Sponge Bread. This bread has a little more "yeasty" flavor than that made by the regular method and is a nice change.

Sponge

1 package active dry yeast
1 cup lukewarm water
1 tablespoon sugar
2 cups all-purpose flour

Combine yeast and water and let stand for 5 minutes. Add sugar and stir in flour, beating to form a smooth, thick batter. Cover tightly and set oven temperature to the left edge of the 150°F setting or between the end of the black line and the 150°F setting. Air should feel warm not hot. Let proof for 30 minutes. Batter should be bubbly; if not, let proof a bit longer.

Dough

1 cup evaporated milk, at room temperature
2 tablespoons sugar
2 teaspoons salt
2 tablespoons softened butter or margarine
4 cups all-purpose flour

Stir down sponge. Add milk, sugar, salt, butter and 2 cups flour. Beat vigorously and add enough remaining flour to make a dough which can be kneaded. Turn dough out on a lightly floured board and knead for 8 to 10 minutes or until smooth and satiny. Put into a greased bowl and turn dough to grease. Put in oven set as for sponge; cover tightly and set timer for 1 hour, or until doubled in bulk. Punch down. Reset timer and let dough rise 30 minutes. Divide dough into 2 parts and let rest, covered, on lightly floured board for 10 minutes. Shape into loaves and put into greased 9 ×5 ×3-inch loaf pans. Grease or oil top of loaves. Let rise in oven set as for sponge for 1 hour or until doubled in bulk. Bake at 300°F for 30 to 40 minutes or until loaves are browned and sound hollow when tapped. **Makes 2 loaves.**

kolaches

Kolaches or Kolacis were what we called "Bohemian" rolls. They were fruit-filled rolls very popular in the Midwest. The 18 rolls are breakfast-size. If you want to make them smaller make 24 to 26 from the recipe.

Filling

1 cup chopped, cooked, pitted prunes
¼ cup sugar
1 tablespoon lemon juice
½ teaspoon cinnamon
¼ teaspoon ground cloves

It takes about 15 large prunes to make 1 cup of chopped, cooked, pitted prunes. Mix all the filling ingredients together, and set aside.

Dough

1 package active dry yeast
½ cup warm milk
¼ cup sugar
½ teaspoon salt
¼ cup soft butter or margarine
1 egg
2½ cups (about) all-purpose flour
Melted butter or margarine
Confectioners' sugar

Combine yeast with milk, sugar, salt, butter, egg and 1 cup flour and beat vigorously. Add remaining flour to make a soft dough. Knead 8 to 10 minutes on a lightly floured board until dough is satiny and smooth. Put into a greased bowl and turn to grease top. Cover tightly. Set temperature to the left edge of the 150°F setting or between the end of the black line and the 150°F setting. Air should feel warm not hot. Let rise until doubled in bulk, about 1 hour. Turn dough out onto floured board. Cut into 18 uniform pieces. Cover and let rest 10 minutes. Then shape into balls and place 3 inches apart on a greased baking sheet. Let rise in oven set for rising until double in bulk. Press down in the center and brush with melted butter. Fill with prune filling. Leave a rim about ¼ inch wide around outside of filling. Return to oven set for rising. Let rise until double in bulk. Bake at 300°F for 15 to 20 minutes, or until nicely browned. Sprinkle with confectioners' sugar while still warm. **Makes 18 rolls.**

easy cheese bread

This cheese bread makes marvelous sandwiches or serves as an accompaniment to salads or soups.

1 package (13¾-ounce) hot roll mix
1 cup lukewarm water
2 eggs, well beaten
½ cup 100% bran cereal
1½ cups (6 ounces) grated Swiss cheese
1 tablespoon caraway seed

Pour yeast from package into a bowl. Add water and stir to dissolve yeast. Stir in eggs, bran and cheese. Add flour from mix and seeds and beat to blend. Knead on floured board until smooth and satiny, about 10 minutes. Put dough in greased bowl, turn to grease dough, cover tightly and let rise in convection oven with temperature set to left edge of 150°F setting or between the end of the black line and the 150°F setting. Air should feel warm not hot. Let rise until doubled in bulk, about 1 hour. Shape into loaf and place in a greased 9 ×5 ×3-inch loaf pan. Return to oven and let rise 30 minutes longer. Bake at 300°F for 30–40 minutes until golden brown. Remove from pan and cool on rack. Do not cut until cooled. **Makes 1 loaf.**

sourdough starter

Sourdough bread is not something made on the spur of the moment, though once the starter is on hand it becomes less of a project. It originated perhaps 4,000 years ago, but became famous in America from the pots of sourdough starter carried by the prospectors in Alaska during the Gold Rush.

Mix **2 cups all-purpose flour** with **1 package active dry yeast** and **2 cups warm water** in a glass or pottery bowl. Cover and place in area free of draft for 48 hours. Stir well before using.

To keep starter going:

Pour out required amount and replenish remaining starter by mixing in **one cup each flour and water.** Let stand uncovered in convection oven with temperature set to left edge of 150°F setting or between the end of the black line and the 150°F setting. Air should feel warm not hot. Let stand for 1 to 1½ hours until starter bubbles. Store, loosely covered in refrigerator. Use and replenish every two weeks.

sourdough bread

1 package active dry yeast
1 cup warm water
1 cup Sourdough Starter—at room temperature
6 cups (about) all-purpose flour
1 tablespoon salt
2 teaspoons sugar
$^1/_2$ teaspoon baking soda
Cornmeal

Dissolve yeast in warm water. Add sourdough starter, 4 cups flour, salt and sugar. Beat for 3 minutes. Cover tightly, and let rise in convection oven with temperature set to left edge of 150°F setting or between the end of the black line and the 150°F setting. Air should feel warm not hot. Let rise for 1 hour or until double in bulk. Mix soda with 1 cup of the remaining flour and stir into dough. Turn dough onto a floured board and knead in remaining flour, using additional flour, if necessary, until dough is smooth and elastic. Shape dough into 2 oblong loaves and place on a greased baking sheet sprinkled with corn-meal. Cover and let rise in convection oven with temperature set for rising until double in size.

To bake:

Place an 8-inch baking pan filled halfway with water on the floor of the oven. Preheat oven to 350°F for 10 minutes. Make several parallel slashes across top of loaves and brush top with water. Place on rack in center of oven. Bake for 25 to 30 minutes or until brown and crusty. **Makes 2 loaves.**

peach cinnamon coffee cake

A moist fruity cake good both warm or cool and easy to make.

2 cups all-purpose flour
$1/3$ cup sugar
2 teaspoons baking powder
$1/2$ teaspoon baking soda
$1/2$ teaspoon salt
$1/2$ teaspoon cinnamon
$1/4$ cup butter or margarine
$3/4$ cup peach juice
1 tablespoon lemon juice
1 egg
1 cup chopped, well drained, canned peaches
3 tablespoons sugar
$1/4$ teaspoon cinnamon

Sift together flour, $1/3$ cup sugar, baking powder, soda, salt and cinnamon into a bowl. With 2 knives or a pastry blender cut in butter until blended. Beat peach and lemon juices and egg together and fold into flour mixture just to blend. Stir in peaches, spoon into a greased and floured 8 ×8 ×2-inch pan. Mix 3 tablespoons sugar with $1/4$ teaspoon cinnamon and sprinkle on batter in pan. Bake at 300°F for 35 minutes. Cool in pan about 5 minutes before cutting. **Makes 1 coffee cake.**

date cheese bread

Good for tea, snacks, sandwiches.

$^3/_4$ **cup apple juice**
1 cup chopped dates
1 $^3/_4$ cups all-purpose flour
$^1/_2$ **cup sugar**
$^1/_2$ **teaspoon salt**
1 teaspoon soda
1 egg, beaten
1 cup grated American cheese
$^3/_4$ **cup chopped walnuts**

Bring apple juice to the boiling point and add dates. Let stand 10 minutes. In a bowl mix flour, sugar, salt and soda to blend. Add date mixture, egg, cheese and nuts, blending well. Spoon into a greased and floured 9 ×5 ×2-inch loaf pan. Bake at 300°F 40 to 45 minutes. Let cool in pan on rack 5 minutes. Carefully remove and cool on rack. When cool, wrap in aluminum foil and store overnight before cutting. **Makes 1 loaf.**

dried apple coffee cake

This is a very tasty way to use some of the apples dried in the convection oven.

2 cups all-purpose flour
2 teaspoons baking powder
$^1/_2$ teaspoon baking soda
$^1/_2$ teaspoon cinnamon
$^1/_4$ teaspoon nutmeg
$^1/_2$ teaspoon salt
$^1/_4$ cup sugar
6 tablespoons butter or margarine
1 egg, beaten
1 cup plain yogurt
$^1/_2$ cup cut-up dried apples
2 tablespoons sugar
$^1/_4$ teaspoon cinnamon

Sift dry ingredients into bowl. Cut butter in with 2 knives or pastry blender. Combine egg and yogurt and stir into dry ingredients just to moisten. Mix in apples. Spread into an 8 ×8 ×2-inch greased and floured pan. Sprinkle top with 2 tablespoons sugar mixed with ¼ teaspoon cinnamon. Bake at 325°F about 30 minutes. Top should spring back when lightly touched with finger. **Makes 1 coffee cake.**

biscuit shortcakes

These shortcakes make a wonderful base for strawberries, peaches, blueberries or any other of your favorite fruits. Split the biscuits, put fruit on bottom half and top with remaining half and some more fruit. Serve with cream, plain or whipped.

2 cups all-purpose flour
3 teaspoons baking powder
$^1/_2$ teaspoon salt
3 tablespoons sugar
6 tablespoons shortening
$^2/_3$ cup milk
4 tablespoons melted butter

Mix flour with other dry ingredients in a bowl. Cut in shortening with a pastry blender or two knives until a fine mixture results. Stir in milk just to moisten all flour. Pat out on a lightly floured surface to ¼-inch thick. Cut half into seven 2½-inch biscuits. Place on baking sheet and spread with melted butter. Cut remaining dough into seven biscuits and place on top of already buttered biscuits. Butter top of these biscuits. Bake at 325°F for 12 to 15 minutes or until nicely browned. **Makes 7 shortcakes.**

Desserts

The convection oven can be used for all kinds of baked desserts as sophisticated as a Soufflé Grand Marnier or as old fashioned as Caramel Bread Pudding.

Most of the desserts in this chapter can be tucked into the oven while the rest of the meal is being prepared. Use a hearty, filling dessert like bread pudding to augment a light meal. Broiled grapefruit halves are perfect for weight watchers.

soufflé grand marnier

A dessert soufflé is spectacular. Remember, the guests must be ready when the soufflé is.

5 tablespoons flour
1/2 cup sugar
1/8 teaspoon salt
1 cup milk
5 egg yolks
4 tablespoons Grand Marnier*
6 egg whites

Combine flour, sugar and salt in a saucepan. Stir in milk gradually. Cook and stir over low heat until mixture is smooth and thick. Beat egg yolks until thick and yellow. Fold into mixture and cool. Fold in liqueur. Beat egg whites until stiff. Fold into egg yolk mixture. Pour into a 1 1/2 -quart soufflé dish which has been buttered and sprinkled with granulated sugar. Bake at 375°F for 25 to 30 minutes. Serve at once. **Makes 4 to 6 servings.**

---

*Or other favorite liqueur.

baked rhubarb sauce

The fresh taste of spring rhubarb enhanced with a touch of orange and raisins becomes a special dessert. Serve in your prettiest glass dessert dishes as a finale to a spring lamb dinner.

1 pound fresh rhubarb
1/2 cup sugar
1/4 cup raisins
1/2 cup orange juice

Wash rhubarb and cut into 1-inch pieces. Put into a 4-cup casserole and add remaining ingredients. Cover and bake at 400°F for about 20 minutes. **Makes about 3 cups.** Serve warm or chilled.

baked pears in wine

A highly popular dessert that can easily be baked along with the rest of your dinner.

6 ripe pears
1 cup dry red wine
½ cup sugar
½ -inch cinnamon stick

Peel the pears, but leave the stem intact. Place in a casserole on their sides. Add wine, sugar and stick cinnamon. Cover and bake at 350°F for about 25 minutes or until tender. Turn pears in wine once during baking. Cool in wine and serve at room temperature or chilled. **Makes 6 servings.**

tropical baked bananas

If baked bananas have not been on your cooking list, you've been missing a rare treat.

4 medium-sized firm bananas
2 tablespoons orange juice
2 tablespoons honey
½ teaspoon cinnamon
2 tablespoons softened butter or margarine
Dairy sour cream or softened vanilla ice cream

Peel bananas, cut in half crosswise, and place in a buttered 8 ×8 ×2-inch pan. Beat together orange juice, honey, cinnamon and butter and spread over bananas. Bake at 400°F for 10 minutes. Serve two halves in dessert dish topped with sour cream or ice cream. **Makes 4 servings.**

Variation:

Dribble **2 tablespoons rum** over bananas before baking.

baked peaches

When fresh peaches are in season, this dessert will be popular. However, well-drained canned peach halves can be baked the same way.

6 ripe peaches
3 tablespoons brown sugar
2 tablespoons butter
4 tablespoons brandy
2 tablespoons water

Peel peaches, cut in half and remove pits. Place in a shallow baking dish. Sprinkle with sugar and dot with butter. Pour brandy over peaches and add water to bottom of pan. Bake at 375°F for 20 minutes or until tender. Serve warm. **Makes 6 servings.**

Variation:
_____

Mix ½ **teaspoon cinnamon** and a dash each of **ground nutmeg** and **cloves** into sugar.

baked spiced applesauce

A dish of this spicy applesauce could go into the oven when some other baking was being done. You might serve this dish with a juicy pork roast.

2 pounds apples (6 to 8, depending on size)
½ cup sugar
1 teaspoon nutmeg
½ teaspoon cinnamon
3 tablespoons water
1 tablespoon lemon juice

Peel and core apples and slice into a buttered 5-cup casserole. Mix sugar and spices and add with water and lemon juice to apples. Cover and bake at 375°F for 25 minutes. The apples should be tender but not mushy. Serve warm or chilled. **Makes 6 servings.**

cranberry apple crisp

Tuck this crunchy good dessert in the oven with roast beef. It will come out bubbling and yummy to serve warm.

1 cup canned whole cranberry sauce
1 cup chopped, peeled apples
$1/2$ cup quick-cooking oatmeal, uncooked
$1/3$ cup firmly packed brown sugar
$1/4$ teaspoon salt
3 tablespoons melted butter or margarine
$1/4$ cup chopped nuts

Mix cranberry sauce and apples together in a buttered 9 × 4-inch loaf pan. Combine remaining ingredients and sprinkle over fruit. Bake at 300°F for 45 minutes. Serve warm with vanilla ice cream, if desired. **Makes 4 servings.**

quick apple custard pie

Made in a quiche pan. This apple custard combination will become a favorite in a hurry.

4 thin slices firm white bread
$1/4$ cup softened butter or margarine
1 cup bread cubes
1 can (1-pound 6-ounce) apple pie filling
$1/2$ cup raisins
6 tablespoons brown sugar
$1/2$ teaspoon cinnamon
$1/4$ teaspoon nutmeg
2 eggs
$1 1/2$ cups milk

Toast bread slices. Spread with part of softened butter and line bottom of a buttered 10-inch quiche pan without removable bottom with toast. Mix bread cubes with remaining butter, apple pie filling and raisins. Spoon into toast-lined dish. In same bowl blend sugar, spices, eggs and milk. Pour over bread-apple mixture in pan. Bake at 300°F for 45 minutes or until center is firm. Cut into pie shaped pieces. Best served warm. **Makes 6 to 8 servings.**

peachy shortcake

A quickly made dessert. If calories are no problem, top each serving with a little ice cream or whipped topping.

1 can (12-ounce) Texas-style refrigerated baking powder biscuits
1 can (1-pound) sliced peaches, well drained
2 tablespoons sugar
$\frac{1}{2}$ teaspoon cinnamon
$\frac{1}{4}$ teaspoon nutmeg
2 tablespoons butter or margarine

Butter well an 8-inch metal pie plate. Cover bottom with 7 biscuits, spreading with fingers to cover pie plate. Fill with peaches, sprinkle with sugar and spices and dot with butter. Flatten remaining biscuits with fingers and arrange around outside edge of peaches. Bake at 350°F 25 minutes or until biscuits are browned. Serve warm cut in wedges. **Makes 6 servings.**

caramel bread pudding

This recipe can easily be cut in half if 10 to 12 servings is too much. It is adapted from a cookbook first printed in 1913—and so good it should be made. Served warm with ice ceam or whipped cream, it's a little reminiscent of Indian Pudding.

3 cups soft bread crumbs
1 quart milk, heated
1 cup granulated sugar
$\frac{1}{4}$ cup brown sugar
2 eggs, well beaten
$\frac{1}{2}$ teaspoon salt
4 tablespoons butter or margarine
1 teaspoon lemon extract
Freshly grated nutmeg to taste

Combine bread crumbs with milk and let stand while caramelizing sugar. Melt granulated sugar in a heavy skillet, stirring constantly, until it turns a light brown. Add at once with remaining ingredients except nutmeg to bread and milk, mixing well. Pour into a well-buttered 1$\frac{3}{4}$-quart casserole and sprinkle with nutmeg. Bake at 300°F for 1$\frac{1}{2}$ hours. Serve warm or cold. **Makes 10 to 12 servings.**

honey rice pudding

A honey of a rice pudding

⅔ **cup uncooked regular rice**
3 cups milk, scalded
¾ **cup honey**
½ **teaspoon salt**
3 eggs, slightly beaten
½ **cup chopped dates or raisins**

Cook rice in boiling salted water until tender, about 15 minutes. Drain and rinse in cold water. Combine rice, milk, honey and salt. Add a little of the hot rice mixture to eggs and return to rice, mixing well. Stir in dates or raisins. Pour into a buttered 6-cup casserole. Bake at 350°F for 60 minutes or until center is firm. Stir once or twice during first 30 minutes of baking.
Makes 6 to 8 servings.

broiled grapefruit halves

Any of these hot grapefruit ideas makes a light, welcome dessert. Take advantage of the broiler to make them when using it for some other broiling.

Cut **grapefruit** in halves crosswise and remove seeds, if any. Cut out core and loosen sections by cutting around with a sharp knife. Entire membrane may be removed, if one wishes. Place grapefruit halves on a flat pan. Sprinkle with **brown sugar** and broil (after preheating for 10 minutes) until hot and bubbly, about 10 minutes. Allow ½ grapefruit per serving.

Variations:

- Add a **spoonful of rum, brandy** or **sherry** to each brown sugared grapefruit.
- Omit sugar and add **a generous dollop of whole cranberry sauce** or **orange marmalade.**
- Omit sugar and pour **green creme de menthe** over grapefruit.
- Omit sugar and pour **maraschino cherry juice** over grapefruit.
  Decorate center of grapefruit with **maraschino cherry** when broiled.

island pudding

Baked puddings such as this are an excellent way to get milk into your family's diet.

3 cups milk
3 teaspoons instant coffee
1 cup water
2 cups soft bread crumbs
2 eggs, beaten
$^1/_2$ cup sugar
1 teaspoon vanilla extract
2 tablespoons softened butter or margarine

Combine milk, instant coffee and water in a saucepan and heat until bubbles appear around edge of pan. Stir to dissolve coffee. Add remaining ingredients and mix well. Pour into a buttered 6-cup casserole. Bake at 350°F for 60 minutes or until center is firm. Serve chilled with chocolate sauce. **Makes 6 to 8 servings.**

Pies/Cakes/Cookies

The circulating heat in the convection oven browns pies, cakes and cookies to perfection more quickly and reliably than an ordinary oven. The recipes in this section are developed especially for the convection oven. If you wish to use your own recipes that contain leavening (yeast, baking soda, baking powder, eggs) decrease the temperature by 75°F, but not lower than 300°F.

In choosing pans for baking these products in the convection oven, shiny aluminum pans are most efficient for cakes and cookies, while dull metal pans work better for pies. The outside finish of the utensil is more important to results than the inside. If using a glass pie pan, set it on an aluminum cookie sheet during baking.

Never bake anything directly on the bottom surface of the oven. Use rack at position one or two when possible and always be sure that there is at least 1-inch air space between the pans and walls of the oven. Baking utensils should not touch each other.

crunchy almond squares

A special cookie for a special occasion.

¹/₄ **cup butter or margarine**
³/₄ **cup light brown sugar, firmly packed**
²/₃ **cup all-purpose flour**
1 egg
¹/₂ **teaspoon vanilla extract**
¹/₂ **cup granulated sugar**
¹/₄ **teaspoon salt**
¹/₂ **teaspoon baking powder**
¹/₂ **cup flaked coconut**
¹/₄ **cup finely chopped blanched almonds**

Cream butter with brown sugar until light and fluffy. Blend in all but 2 tablespoons of the flour and spread mixture over the bottom of a greased 8 ×8 ×2-inch pan. Bake at 300°F 10 minutes. Meanwhile, beat egg, vanilla, granulated sugar and salt until fluffy and thick. Fold in 2 tablespoons flour, baking powder, coconut and almonds. Spread over base in pan and continue baking at 300°F for 20 minutes or until center is browned. Cool and cut into small squares. **Makes about 36.**

applesauce bars

A moist bar cookie that keeps well, is good with milk, ice cream or fruit.

1¹/₄ **cups light brown sugar, firmly packed**
³/₄ **cup butter or margarine at room temperature**
1 cup canned applesauce
1 egg
1 teaspoon vanilla extract
2 cups all-purpose flour
1 teaspoon baking soda
¹/₂ **teaspoon each cinnamon and nutmeg**
¹/₂ **teaspoon salt**
¹/₄ **teaspoon cloves**
1 cup raisins
¹/₂ **cup uncooked oatmeal**
¹/₂ **cup chopped nuts**

Cream sugar and butter. Beat in applesauce, egg and vanilla. Stir flour and soda with spices and salt and blend into applesauce mixture. Mix in raisins, oatmeal and nuts. Spread into a greased 15 ×10 ×1-inch pan. Bake at 300°F for 20 minutes. Cool. Cut into bars. **Makes 40 bars.**

orange thins

Cookies to make for a tea or to serve with a fruit or ice cream dessert.

2 eggs
1/4 cup melted butter or margarine
2/3 cup sugar
2 teaspoons grated orange rind
1 tablespoon orange juice
1/2 cup all-purpose flour
1 1/2 teaspoons baking powder
1/4 teaspoon salt
2 1/4 cups soft bread crumbs

Beat eggs until light. Stir in melted butter. Add sugar gradually and mix well. Mix in orange rind and juice. Mix together flour, baking powder and salt. Fold with bread crumbs into egg mixture. Drop by teaspoonfuls 2″ apart on greased cookie sheet. Bake at 325°F about 10 minutes or until lightly browned. **Makes 2 1/2 dozen.**

pumpkin cookies

These spicy good cookies are moist and flavorful. One can use canned pumpkin or the oven steamed pumpkin in the vegetable section of this book (page 71).

1/2 cup shortening
1 1/4 cups firmly packed brown sugar
2 eggs
1 1/2 cups oven steamed (or canned) pumpkin
1 teaspoon vanilla extract
1 teaspoon lemon extract
2 1/2 cups all-purpose flour
4 teaspoons baking powder
1/2 teaspoon salt
1 1/4 teaspoons pumpkin pie spice
1 cup chopped raisins
1 cup chopped nuts

Combine shortening, sugar and eggs, and beat until light and fluffy. Fold in pumpkin and flavorings. (Mixture will look curdled.) Sift flour with dry ingredients and fold into creamed mixture. Stir in raisins and nuts. Chill batter several hours or overnight. Drop by teaspoonfuls on greased baking sheets. Bake at 325°F for 10 to 12 minutes. **Makes about 5 dozen cookies.**

whole wheat walnut cookies

Make today, bake tomorrow, for these crispy good cookies.

$1/2$ **cup shortening**
1 cup sugar
2 eggs
$1/2$ **teaspoon vanilla extract**
$1^3/4$ **cups whole wheat flour**
$1/4$ **teaspoon baking soda**
$1/2$ **teaspoon salt**
$1/2$ **cup finely chopped walnuts**

Combine shortening, sugar, eggs and vanilla and beat until light and fluffy. Mix remaining ingredients and blend into creamed mixture. Shape into a roll. Cover with waxed paper or transparent wrap and chill overnight in the refrigerator. Slice very thin and bake on ungreased cookie sheet at 325°F for 8 to 10 minutes. **Makes 4$^1/2$ dozen.**

Note: 1/4 **cup raisins** added to this recipe will add extra nutrients and flavor.

prune fingers

Another teatime treat and a delicious recipe in which to use those dried prunes.

2 eggs, beaten
$1/2$ **cup smooth peanut butter**
$2/3$ **cup maple flavored syrup**
1 cup cooked prunes, pitted and finely chopped
$1^1/4$ **cups fine graham cracker crumbs**
$1/2$ **teaspoon baking powder**
$1/4$ **teaspoon salt**
Confectioners' sugar

Gradually add eggs to peanut butter, beating well. Beat in syrup and prunes. Mix remaining ingredients and fold into syrup mixture. Pour into greased and waxed paper-lined 8 ×8 ×2-inch pan. Bake at 300°F about 25 to 30 minutes. Remove from pan at once and pull off paper. Cut into finger-length pieces and roll in confectioners' sugar. **Makes about 2 dozen.**

date cookie surprises

These dainty little packages make a nice holiday treat.

3 to 4 dozen pitted dates
¼ cup chopped walnuts (about)
¼ cup butter or margarine
¾ cup firmly packed brown sugar
½ teaspoon vanilla extract
1 egg
1¾ cups all-purpose flour
½ teaspoon salt
¼ teaspoon baking powder
½ teaspoon baking soda
½ cup dairy sour cream

Stuff pitted dates with chopped walnuts and keep covered while making batter Beat together butter, sugar, vanilla and egg until light and fluffy. Sift flour with dry ingredients and add alternately with sour cream to creamed mixture. Dip each date in batter and place on a buttered cookie sheet. Bake at 300°F for 10 minutes. Cool and frost with Confectioners' Sugar Icing.

Confectioners' Sugar Icing:

Mix ¼ **cup butter** or **margarine** with **1 cup sifted confectioners' sugar** and ½ **teaspoon vanilla extract.** Beat in **a few drops of hot water** until mixture is of spreading consistency. **Makes 3 or 4 dozen.**

aunt edith's christmas cookies

Decorated Christmas Cookies always add a gala touch to the holiday festivity. With a good sugar cookie as a base different shapes and colors of frosting make for variety.

1 cup shortening
2 cups sugar
4 eggs
1 teaspoon vanilla or lemon extract
4 cups all-purpose flour
1 teaspoon baking soda
$^1/_2$ teaspoon salt

Cream shortening and sugar until light and fluffy. Beat in eggs and flavoring. Sift together flour, soda and salt and fold into shortening mixture. Divide into 4 parts and wrap each in plastic wrap. Chill overnight or longer. Work with one part at a time, and roll out on a well floured board, or preferably on a pastry cloth with a cloth-covered rolling pin. Cut cookies with assorted Christmas cookie cutters. If the finished cookies are to be hung, make a hole with a sharp pointed knife at point where string will be inserted after cookie has been put on baking sheet, but before baking. Sprinkle with plain or colored sugar before baking, if desired. Bake at 325°F for 8 to 10 minutes or just until cookies begin to brown on edges. Transfer baked cookies to cake rack. Use cookie cutters shaped as stars, Santa, bells, candy canes, wreaths (doughnut cutters can be used to make wreaths). Plain round cookies can become Christmas ornaments. One can make patterns from thin cardboard and cut around them in lieu of cookie cutters. This recipe **makes about 6 dozen cookies.** The dough left from cutting can be rechilled and reworked. You will also note that the recipe can be easily divided to make 3 dozen cookies.

decorator frosting

To decorate the cookies:

3 egg whites
2$\frac{1}{2}$ cups sifted confectioners' sugar (about)
1 teaspoon lemon juice
1$\frac{1}{2}$ tablespoons vegetable shortening
Food coloring
Sprinkles (both chocolate and other colors)
Cinnamon candies
Colored sugars

Beat egg whites and about $\frac{1}{3}$ of sugar with electric mixer for 10 minutes. Add $\frac{1}{3}$ more sugar and lemon juice and beat for 10 minutes longer. Add vegetable shortening and enough extra sugar to make frosting hold an edge when lifted with a spoon. This frosting can be divided into 3 or 4 parts. Leave one white. Tint others red, green, yellow. The frosting can be spread on the cookies with small spatulas or piped on with a cake decorator. Let your imagination take over and have fun. Keep frostings covered with a lightly dampened piece of paper toweling during the decorating. Add any sprinkles, etc., at once after putting frosting on cookies. This frosting is designed to set up and hold its shape. This amount of frosting **will decorate about 4 dozen cookies**, depending on how elaborately it is spread.

apple torte pie

Since apples are available year 'round, now one can make all kinds of apple pies. This one is particularly tasty.

$^3/_4$ **cup sugar**
$^1/_4$ **cup chopped nuts**
$^1/_4$ **teaspoon salt**
1 teaspoon baking powder
$^1/_3$ **cup flour**
1 egg, beaten
2 cups chopped, peeled apples
An 8- or 9-inch unbaked pie shell

Combine sugar, nuts, salt, baking powder and flour, mixing well. Stir in **egg** and apples. Spoon into pie shell. Bake at 300°F for 45 minutes. Serve warm or cold. **Makes 1 apple torte.**

lattice cranberry-pineapple pie

A fruity combination which makes a pretty picture with a lattice top. Also good!

1 recipe for 2 crust pastry
1 cup sugar
2 tablespoons flour
$^1/_2$ **teaspoon cinnamon**
$^1/_8$ **teaspoon salt**
2 cups chopped fresh cranberries
1 cup canned crushed pineapple, drained
2 tablespoons butter or margarine

Roll out bottom crust and fit it into a 9-inch metal pie plate. Mix sugar with flour, cinnamon and salt. Sprinkle half into bottom of pie crust. Mix cranberries and pineapple and spoon into crust. Sprinkle remaining sugar mixture over fruit and dot with butter. Roll out remaining pastry into a 9-inch circle. With a pastry cutter or knife cut into narrow strips. Arrange half strips over filling 1-inch apart and remainder of strips in the opposite way to form a diamond pattern like a lattice. Seal strips to rim of pie and flute edge. Bake at 375°F for 50 minutes or until nicely browned. **Makes 1 pie.**

easy brownie pie

If the ingredients for this dessert are kept on hand, it's easy to pull a fancy one out-of-the-hat when necessary.

1 package (8 ounce) brownie mix
1 egg
1 tablespoon water
1 teaspoon vanilla extract
½ cup chopped nuts
An 8- or 9-inch frozen pie crust, defrosted
1 cup frozen whipped topping, defrosted

Combine brownie mix with egg, water, vanilla and nuts and mix well. Spread into pie crust. Bake at 350°F for 30 minutes. Cool to room temperature. Spread with whipped topping. **Makes 6 servings.**

baked cherry shortcake

Served warm with a little whipped cream or ice cream, this is a luscious dessert. Let it brighten up a soup and sandwich meal.

1½ cups all-purpose flour
1 cup sugar
2 teaspoons baking powder
½ teaspoon cinnamon
¼ teaspoon salt
½ cup butter or margarine
1 egg
1 cup milk
½ teaspoon vanilla extract
1 can (1-pound 5-ounce) cherry pie filling*

Grease and flour an 8 ×8 ×2-inch pan well. Sift dry ingredients into a medium bowl. Cut in butter with 2 knives or pastry blender until well blended. Combine egg, milk and vanilla and add to flour mixture, stirring just to blend. Pour batter into prepared pan. Spoon cherry pie filling over cake. Bake at 300°F for 45 minutes. Serve warm. **Makes 8 servings.**

---

*Pineapple pie filling may be substituted for cherry.

lemon cake ring

When you want a lovely-to-look-at dessert, Lemon Cake Ring is the answer. It combines cake, strawberries and ice cream in favorite flavors.

1 package (18½-ounce) lemon cake mix
1 package (3-ounce) lemon flavor gelatin
4 eggs
⅔ cup milk
⅔ cup vegetable oil
1 quart strawberries
Sugar
1 pint vanilla ice cream

Combine cake mix, gelatin, eggs, milk and vegetable oil in a bowl and beat at medium speed until batter is smooth, about 4 minutes. Grease and flour two 1¼-quart ring molds or one 10-inch angel cake pan. Spoon in batter. Bake ring molds at 300°F for 30 minutes, angel cake pan at 300°F for 40 minutes. Test for doneness by inserting a cake tester or toothpick. If it comes out clean, the cake is done. Cool in pan on rack 10 minutes. Then invert on plate. Cool. To serve, clean strawberries, slice and sweeten with sugar. Fill center of rings with ice cream and top with strawberries. The two rings will serve 12 people. If only one is needed, reduce amount of strawberries and ice cream. Freeze one ring for future use. If cake is baked in an angel cake pan, serve slices with ice cream and strawberries. **Makes 10 to 12 servings.**

danish pound cake

Cardamom is a spice used a great deal at Christmas, but this cake is so good you'll enjoy it anytime. Slice thinly and serve with tea or wine. It freezes well, too.

1 package (1-pound) golden pound cake mix
²/₃ cup plain yogurt
2 eggs
1 teaspoon ground cardamom
Soft bread crumbs

Combine pound cake, yogurt and eggs, beating until smooth. Fold in ground cardamom. Grease well a 9 ×5 ×4-inch loaf pan and cover with soft bread crumbs. Spoon in batter. Bake at 300°F for 1 hour or until cake springs back when touched with finger. Cool in pan on rack for 10 minutes. Turn out on rack and cool. If possible, let cake stand overnight before cutting. Wrap in aluminum foil or transparent wrap to store. **Makes 1 pound cake.**

south american wine cake

This is a special cake for an extraordinary occasion.

2 cups all-purpose flour
1 cup cornstarch
2 teaspoons baking soda
1 teaspoon salt
$1/2$ teaspoon freshly ground nutmeg
1 cup butter or margarine
2 cups sugar
2 tablespoons grated fresh lemon rind
1 cup milk
$1/2$ cup port wine
7 egg whites
Wine sauce
Confectioners' sugar

Grease and flour a 12-cup Bundt pan. Sift together flour, cornstarch, soda, salt and nutmeg. Beat together butter, sugar and fresh lemon rind until well blended, using medium speed on mixer. Fold in sifted dry ingredients alternately with milk, beginning and ending with dry ingredients. Gradually beat in wine. (Mixture will look curdled.) Beat egg whites until stiff peaks form and gently fold into cake batter. Pour into the prepared Bundt pan. Bake at 300°F for 60 minutes or until cake springs back when lightly touched with the fingertip. Cool in pan on rack 10 minutes. Remove from pan and cool. Pour a little of the Wine Sauce* over the cake and sprinkle with confectioners' sugar.

*Wine Sauce:

Mix **1 tablespoon cornstarch** and $1/2$ **cup port wine** until smooth. Gradually beat in $1/2$ **cup red currant jelly.** Cook and stir over medium heat until mixture boils, then cook 1 minute. Cool. **Makes 2 cups.**

The Convection Oven as a Dehydrator

When you purchased a convection oven, you purchased the beginnings of a food dehydrator. With the addition of dehydration racks—you're in business!

Dehydrating (or drying)—removing the moisture from foods—is one of the oldest means of food preservation. Sun drying was the first form of dehydrating and is still used in many sections of the country. However, dehydrating in a convection oven is much more convenient, sanitary and always available, and at a very minimal cost.

why dehydrate foods?

Dehydrated foods require little storage space and no special containers. You can store them in tightly sealed plastic bags or any other clean, air-tight container. This makes them readily available as a source of food any time there is a need. Drying foods while they are in plentiful supply and less expensive is money saving. It not only saves you money but gives a greater variety of foods all year round. For campers or hikers, it is a convenient way to take food for outdoor trail eating or camper cooking. Dried foods, properly stored, will keep up to a year.

what to dehydrate?

Almost anything! Fruits can be used to make some of the fruit "leathers" that are such nutritious snacks. Apples, peaches, berries or any other seasonal fruit can be dried for year round snacking. Almost anything that suits your taste can be dehydrated.

Vegetables can be dried and packed singly or in combinations to add to soups and stews. Use vegetables from your garden or from a local farm stand. Herbs from your garden should be dehydrated and packed singly or in combinations for spaghetti sauce, stews, chicken dishes. What a wonderful gift a jar of your own home grown and dried herbs would make!

There are also craft items that can be dried. Potpourris or sachets can be made from flowers from your spring garden. The use of the convection oven for dehydrating is practically limitless.

There is no mystery about drying foods. In fact most of us eat dried foods every day. Generally, pasta, beans, spices, raisins and even coffee are dried when we buy them.

general instructions

- Dry only good quality fruits and vegetables. The one exception to this is in making fruit leathers. Here you can cut away pieces of the fruit that are spoiled, use up fruits from the freezer that have overstayed their time, even canned fruits that have been hanging around too long.

- The thinner the slices, the faster the drying.

- Place food one layer thick on the trays. Different kinds of foods can be dried at the same time, but it is wise not to mix onion and onion products with less pungent foods such as fruits.

- Leave the oven door open open about 1 inch during drying.

● The majority of foods dry between 140° and 150°F. Set the temperature dial to a point between the "1" and the "5" of the 150°F setting or between the end of the black line and before the 150°F setting.

● During the drying period check oven periodically to make sure temperature is not too high. Scorching could result from too high a temperature.

● Testing for doneness depends a great deal on the variety of fruits and vegetables as well as thickness.

Generally, vegetables are dried when they have become leathery or brittle. Fruits should be leathery and pliable and should not exhibit any moisture when squeezed. Meats will be dark in color when properly dried and form sharp points when bent. Herbs and leaf-type plants will become brittle and crumble easily when fully dried. It is better to overdry than to underdry.

● Drying times on some products like apricots and grapes are quite long. If you wish to use the oven for some other baking or broiling, remove the food on the drying racks to a place where they will be kept clean and away from moisture. When the other cooking is finished, allow the oven to return to low heat (10 or 15 minutes) and continue with the drying. Don't interrupt drying process for too long.

preparation of fruits and vegetables for drying

Fruits may or may not be treated with an ascorbic acid solution before drying. If a fruit such as apples or bananas has a tendency to darken, dip it in a solution of 1 teaspoon ascorbic acid to 1 quart water. (Ascorbic acid, otherwise known as Vitamin C, can be purchased at drugstores or where freezing supplies are sold.) If you prefer, you can brush the fruit with lemon juice. Some berries, such as blueberries, will dry faster if steamed just enough to break the skin.

Vegetables, with the exception of onions, garlic, peppers, tomatoes and mushrooms should be blanched in boiling water as is done in preparation of food for freezing. Drain the blanched vegetables well and put on trays to dry. This blanching process stops enzymatic action and means that the dried vegetables will be of better quality and will keep longer.

drying chart

FRUITS	PREPARATION	DRYING TIME (Hours)	TEST FOR DRYNESS
Apples	Peel, core, cut in 1/8-inch slices	4–8	Pliable, leathery
Apricots*	Pit and half	18–24	Pliable, leathery
Bananas	1/8-inch slices	8–12	Leathery
Blueberries	Steam to break skin	24–28	Pliable, leathery
Grapes	Leave whole	24–28	Pliable, leathery
Nectarines and Peaches*	Pit and half	24–36	Pliable, leathery
Pears*	Peel, core and slice	10–24	Pliable, leathery
Plums*	Pit and half	18–36	Pliable, leathery
Rhubarb	Slice 1/4-inch thick	5–8	Leathery
Strawberries	Slice 1/8-inch thick	6–8	Pliable

*To reduce the drying time, press onto board and flatten to remove excess moisture

VEGETABLES	PREPARATION	DRYING TIME (HOURS)	TEST FOR DRYNESS
Green beans	Cut in pieces	4–6	Brittle
Beets	Cook, cut in thin strips or slices	3–5	Brittle
Broccoli	Cut stems in quarters	3–9	Brittle
Cabbage	Cut into thin slices	3–8	Brittle
Carrots	1/4-inch slices	4–8	Brittle
Celery	1/4-inch slices	3–6	Brittle
Fresh Corn	Cut off cob	4–6	Dry, brittle
Mushrooms	Slice 1/4-inch thick	3–6	Leathery
Onions	Slice 1/8 to 1/4-inch thick	3–9	Brittle
Peas	Shell	8–12	Wrinkled
Peppers*	Remove core, white ribs and seeds, slice 1/4-inch	2–6	Brittle
Spinach, other greens	Trim, wash	3–8	Brittle
Squash	Strip or slices, 1/4-inch	4–10	Brittle
Tomatoes	Remove skins by dipping in boiling water. Cut into 1/4–1/2-inch slices	6–10	Leathery

*For hot peppers such as Jalapeño, leave in the seeds for a hotter pepper

HERBS	PREPARATION	DRYING TIME (HOURS)	TEST FOR DRYNESS
All herb leaves should be dried on stem, when possible. There is no special preparation, except if the herbs are dusty, rinse in cold water and dry. All herbs can be dried including parsley, chives, and basil.		2–6 hours	Brittle

Fruit leathers are one of my favorite things to be made in the convection oven. They are a combination of fruits, nuts, if desired, and honey or corn syrup to sweeten slightly. The mixture of fruits is puréed in a food processor or blender and blended with the honey or corn syrup. If nuts are used, they should be chopped fine, but do not have to be puréed. Honey or corn syrup is not essential as fruit sweetens naturally when dried. Spread on a piece of plastic wrap taped to the tray, they dry to a leather consistency, from which comes the name. Vegetables can also be made into leathers.

Fruit leathers make a fine, nutritious snack and are an excellent item for campers or hikers.

Each of the drying trays in the convection oven will hold 1¾ -2 cups of puréed fruit.

directions for fruit leather

Wash, clean and prepare enough fruit (to prepare fruit means to peel, remove hulls, pits, etc.) to make 1¾ cups puréed fruit. Generally speaking, it takes about twice as much prepared fruit to make 1¾ cups puree. Add 1 to 2 tablespoons honey or corn syrup to mixture if desired. If you are using banana, you might want to also add 1 tablespoon of lemon juice to retard darkening. Cover a dehydrator rack with a piece of plastic wrap. Tape corners of plastic wrap securely to corners of rack. Spread puréed fruit evenly on rack and put in oven. Set temperature dial at 150°F and timer at STAY ON. Leave door open 1 inch. Dry 6 to 8 hours or until no longer sticky to touch of finger.

When leather is dry, carefully peel off plastic wrap. (At this stage some directions say to dry the leather 1 hour longer. If the bottom feels sticky, do so.)

Roll leather from long side and wrap in plastic wrap, twisting ends to seal. A tie on each end will assure a secure seal. Store in a cool dark dry place or in freezer. Do not store in the refrigerator. It will keep for 6 months or longer.

When ready to use, fruit leathers can be cut in bar-size pieces for easier use in school lunch boxes or backpacks.

Try some combinations such as:

> Honey warmed with nuts or seeds, coconut and some uncooked oatmeal, enough to make a spreadable mixture.
>
> Blueberries and peaches
>
> Blueberries and oranges
>
> Rhubarb and strawberries
>
> Fresh pineapple and banana

Fruit chips are made like fruit leathers, except they are dried to crispness so that they can be broken or cut into chips. They are best made with fruits that have a naturally sweet flavor. Apples, nectarines, peaches, pineapples and strawberries would be among the choices. Do not add any sweetening.

Purée as with leathers and pour on the plastic wrap-lined tray. Dry until top side is smooth with no soft spots. Then pull off plastic wrap and dry the back for at least another hour. The whole process can take 6 to 24 hours, primarily depending on how much liquid is in the original purée. The fruit chip should be crisp and will break easily.

Other uses for leathers and chips:

The leathers can be cut into small pieces and ground up in the food processor (steel blade) or blender and used as a topping for ice cream, in yogurt, or made into a syrup.

Fruit Syrup From Fruit Leather:

Combine **one ground-up leather** with $\frac{1}{2}$ **cup corn syrup or honey** and $\frac{1}{4}$ **cup water.** Cook, stirring, over low heat for about 5 minutes. **Makes $\frac{2}{3}$ cup.** Good for milk shakes or over ice cream.

recipes

If using dried fruit in a recipe, use half as much as you would fresh fruit. Generally, rehydrate with equal parts water or a compatible fruit juice. Depending on shape of fruit (shredded, grated, sliced, whole), the rehydrating can take from 15 minutes to 3 hours.

fruit soup

1 cup pitted dried prunes
1 cup dried pear slices
1 cup dried apple slices
1 quart water or fruit juice
$\frac{1}{2}$ cup sugar
A 2-inch cinnamon stick
2 tablespoons lemon juice
1 teaspoon grated lemon rind
1 tablespoon cornstarch

Soak fruit in water 2 to 3 hours. Add sugar and cinnamon stick and cook over low heat until tender, about 30 minutes. Add lemon juice, rind and cornstarch mixed with 2 tablespoons water. Bring to a boil, stirring. Chill. Serve as a first course or dessert. **Makes 4 to 6 servings.**

gelatin dessert

Add **dried fruits** to **fruit gelatin** after it has been dissolved according to package directions. The fruit will rehydrate as gelatin sets. About 1 cup dried fruit is enough for a **4-serving package.**

dessert dumplings

1 cup cut up dried fruit
3 cups water
¼ cup sugar
2 tablespoons butter or margarine
2 cups buttermilk biscuit mix
2 tablespoons sugar
1 tablespoon butter or margarine
⅔ cup milk

Combine fruit with water and let stand overnight in the refrigerator. When ready to cook, bring to a boil with ¼ cup sugar and 2 tablespoons butter and simmer, covered, until tender, 30 to 40 minutes. Mix biscuit mix with 2 tablespoons sugar and 1 tablespoon butter. Fold in milk just to blend. Drop by spoonfuls on top of hot fruit. Cook, uncovered, 10 minutes. Cover and cook 10 minutes longer. Serve hot. **Makes 4 to 6 servings.**

Other Uses For Dried Fruits:

Cut up dried fruits can be added to cookies, breads, muffins. They can be rehydrated and cooked to serve as sauces. Once you get into drying you will find myriad ways to use the products.

vegetable recipes

Soak **vegetables** in equal parts of **water** to rehydrate. The way in which the vegetable is prepared, i.e. shredded, sliced, etc., determines the length of time for rehydration. Add more water if vegetable is to be served as a vegetable, not an ingredient in a recipe. Salt at end of cooking time.

zucchini sausage casserole

1 $^1/_2$ **cups dried shredded zucchini**
1 $^1/_2$ **cups water**
$^1/_4$ **cup dried chopped onion**
6 sausage links
1 can (10$^1/_2$ -ounce) condensed cream of mushroom soup
2 eggs, beaten
$^1/_2$ **cup mayonnaise**
$^3/_4$ **cup milk**
1 cup grated cheese

Combine zucchini, water and onion and soak overnight in the refrigerator. Sauté sausage links until lightly browned. Set aside. Mix soup with remaining ingredients and stir in squash and onion. Spoon into a buttered 6-cup casserole. Arrange sausage on top. Bake at 375°F for 50 minutes or until bubbly. **Makes 4 to 6 servings.**

Dried vegetables are marvelous to have ready as a soup mix. Combine your own favorite soup vegetables, and store in soup pot amounts or put in pretty jars and give as a gift. Generally speaking the vegetable doubles in quantity when cooked.

herbs

Herbs take about 2 to 6 hours to dry depending on thickness of leaves. If you raise your own or can buy them that way, dry leaves on stem. (Tie bundles of the dried stems together and hang in the garage, attic and other out of the way places for a pleasing odor.) The only reason for drying herbs on the stem is because they are much easier to handle that way and in the case of small leaves like thyme, will not fall through the mesh. Herbs stored as whole leaves, however, retain flavor longer. Store in airtight containers to maintain the aroma. When ready to use, they can be crumbled or powdered.

Make up combinations of herbs to use in particular dishes.

A fish herb combination might contain equal parts of parsley, celery leaves, thyme, marjoram and a little less than equal part of chives.

For poultry, parsley, oregano, thyme, rosemary, celery leaves, and sage. Go a little heavier on the thyme and rosemary and less of the sage.

A spaghetti sauce mix could be equal parts of oregano, thyme and basil with a little hot pepper thrown in if you like it.

Experiment to make your own specials.

The convection oven as a dehydrator is a money saver. Fresh parsley is expensive, but has so many uses in cooking that I like to keep it on hand. I keep my eye on it and the minute I see one yellow leaf, it is headed for the oven, so that there is always parsley on hand, dried or fresh. The same with celery leaves. Dry them so that when the price of celery goes out of sight, the dried leaves can be used to give the celery flavor to cooking. These things one can do to add interest and save money in cooking even if one does not take the time to dry the whole vegetable.

jerky

Another dehydrator special is jerky. Originally it was a product of the hard life in the plains states when our country was being settled. Then the flesh of game animals was dried in the sun to preserve it for future days. Nowadays it serves both as hiking or a cocktail party specialty.

The meat used in jerky can be beef, venison, elk, bison or antelope. It must be boneless and cut in strips from 1 to 2-inches thick. Be certain to remove all fat. Freeze this meat for about 1 hour and slice it *with* the grain (opposite of cutting steaks) into slices no thicker than 1/4-inch. There are people who recommend cutting the meat with the grain as you do a steak. The difference in the end product is that the jerky cut with the grain has a tendency to be a little tougher to chew and will not break as easily after being dried.

Lay the strips on the drying rack quite close, since they shrink as they dry. Sprinkle with a goodly coating of seasoned salt.

Set the oven temperature at 150°F and leave the door open about 1 inch.

About 18 hours are required to dry the jerky. It will be nearly black and when pieces are broken there will be no interior moisture showing.

Store in covered containers in the refrigerator or the freezer, or keep the jerky in the covered containers in a cool, dark place. From five pounds of meat you will get about 1 pound of jerky.

crafts

The dehydrator as a helpful hand in your craft projects is unending. It can be used to dry flowers for winter bouquets. It dries such things as beads made from rose petals or paper. Applehead dolls can be dried in the oven. Products from the various craft doughs dry more quickly and are dust free when dried in the oven. Here are a couple of suggestions. If you enjoy making crafts, you will find many more ideas.

potpourri

If possible, pick petals from the rose when they are newly opened or are unopened buds. They are most fragrant then. However, since today's roses are grown for color and size rather than fragrance, it is wise to add blossoms such as stock, rose geranium, lavender or lemon verbena to the rose petals.

Spread the rose petals on the trays along with the other blossoms and let dry until crisp. If you want to make several potpourri jars save the petals as they dry in a plastic bag or covered container until you have enough. The actual bulk of the dried petals will be only about ⅓ to ¼ of the amount of fresh petals. The time of drying varies from 7 to 20 hours depending on the thickness of the petals on flowers.

To make the Potpourri:

In a large bowl combine **1 quart dried rose petals** (or rose petals and whatever combination of flowers you have dried) with about **4 tablespoons of powdered orris root,** ½ **teaspoon each ground cloves, cinnamon, allspice, coriander and mace** (or any other combination of these if you do not wish to use all). Add **a few drops of oil of lavender, rose or violet.** Stir the mixture until the orris root, spices and scented oil are well mixed throughout the petals. Fill into whatever containers you have chosen and cover tightly.

Orris root and the fragrant oils can be purchased in drugstores. The orris root acts as a fixative to hold the fragrance for a longer time. Sometimes bits of dried lemon or orange peel are added. Fresh ground or crushed spices give a headier bouquet. Also helpful in making a longer lasting fragrant jar is the addition of a few drops of brandy at the time of mixing and then remembering to add a few drops every six to eight months.

Besides putting the potpourri in jars, it can be sewn into little bags to perfume the drawers which contain lingerie, sheets and similar items.

Cooking for One or Two

More and more households are comprised of only one or two people. Cooking in small quantities can pose a problem from time to time. Let your convection oven solve your problems. Cook your entire meal in the convection oven.

The ingredients in most casserole recipes can be decreased proportionately. For example, if the recipe calls for three eggs, halve the recipe by using two small eggs. Remember that a cup equals sixteen tablespoons. That will help when dividing ⅓ cup or ¼ cup in half. Many products like tuna and soup are now sold in individual servings.

Any leftovers you might have can be frozen, refrigerated a day or two—or taken to work the next day for lunch.

Recipes in this chapter are designed for one or two people. Who said you need a large crowd to eat well?

kebabs for one or two

Lightly dressed crisp raw spinach will complement this meal of Kebabs, cannellini beans and grilled tomatoes. Served sliced oranges sprinkled with Kirsch for dessert. The amounts in this meal may easily be cut in half for one person.

$^1/_2$ **pound cubed lamb**
2 teaspoons instant minced onion
$^1/_2$ **cup dry white wine**
2 tablespoons olive oil
$^1/_4$ **teaspoon salt**
4 or 6 pineapple chunks
4 or 6 stuffed olives
1 cup cooked cannellini beans
1 teaspoon chopped chives
1 teaspoon chopped fresh basil or $^1/_2$ teaspoon dried
2 tablespoons chopped fresh parsley
1 tomato, cut in half crosswise
Bread crumbs
Butter or margarine

Combine lamb with onion, wine, olive oil and salt and let marinate several hours or overnight in the refrigerator. When ready to cook, alternate lamb cubes with pineapple and olives on two skewers. Combine cannellini beans with chives, basil and parsley and spoon into a small casserole and cover. Cut tomatoes in half crosswise and sprinkle with bread crumbs and dot with butter.

To cook:

Put drip pan and rack in bottom position and set beans on one side of shelf. Preheat oven for 10 minutes at "BROIL" or 450°F. Broil kebabs 10 to 15 minutes. Put tomatoes on shelf about 5 minutes before kebabs are done.

chicken cutlet dinner for two

Here we have the whole dinner broiled at once. An apple salad could serve as both salad and dessert to fill out the menu.

½ **pound chicken or turkey cutlets**
Flour
1 egg
1 tablespoon water
½ **cup fine, dry bread crumbs**
¼ **teaspoon salt**
Freshly ground pepper to taste
1 medium zucchini squash
2 medium tomatoes
3 to 4 tablespoons melted butter or margarine
Seasoned salt
Parmesan cheese
½ **half loaf (or less) buttered French bread**

Cut chicken cutlets into 2 servings and pound them between wax paper or transparent wrap. Dip in flour, then in egg mixed with water and finally in crumbs seasoned with salt and pepper. Allow to stand at room temperature about 30 minutes. Meanwhile, cook zucchini in water to cover for 5 minutes and cut in half lengthwise. Cut about ½-inch off tops of tomatoes. Preheat oven to "BROIL" or 450°F for 10 minutes. Place chicken cutlets on rack over drip pan and spoon melted butter over them. Place tomatoes and zucchini on rack. Sprinkle tomatoes with seasoned salt, zucchini with Parmesan cheese. Wrap bread in foil and place in oven. Put rack and drip tray in oven at floor position and broil 8 to 10 minutes. **Makes dinner for 2.**

meal-in-one stuffed squash

A favorite combination will be this meal-in-one Stuffed Squash and muffins. Start the meal with tomato juice spiked with fresh lime juice. Radishes and celery sticks double for salad, Neapolitan ice cream squares for dessert.

1 large acorn squash
1 link sweet Italian sausage, casing removed
1 tablespoon butter or margarine
1 small onion, chopped
1 small apple, peeled and chopped
1 cup shredded cabbage
1 tablespoon slivered almonds
¼ teaspoon salt
Dash dried thyme
Dash dried leaf sage
1 package (8-ounce) muffin mix of your choice

Wash and cut squash in half lengthwise and remove seeds. Place in a baking pan with ½-inch water. Bake at 350°F for 20 minutes. While squash is baking cook sausage meat in skillet until browned. Drain off excess fat and add butter, onion, apple, cabbage, almonds and seasonings and cook and stir until vegetables are tender. Turn squash cut side up and fill centers with mixture. Continue baking at 350°F for 25 to 30 minutes. Prepare muffin mix as directed and bake at 350°F for required length of time while squash is baking. **Makes dinner for 2.**

zucchini casserole for two

Bake two apples while zucchini is baking and heat some canned peas and chopped celery in a covered casserole to serve with the squash casserole.

1/2 **pound pork sausage**
1/4 **cup chopped onion**
1/4 **cup chopped green pepper**
1/2 **cup 100% bran cereal**
1/4 **teaspoon poultry seasoning**
1/2 **cup dairy sour cream**
2 medium zucchini squash
Salt
Freshly ground black pepper
4 ounces sliced mozzarella cheese
2 tablespoons grated Parmesan cheese

Pan fry sausage until lightly browned and crumbled into small pieces. Drain off most of fat and saute onion and pepper until tender, but not browned. Toss with sausage, cereal and poultry seasoning; blend in sour cream. Remove ends from zucchini and slice lengthwise and thinly as possible. Line bottom of 8 ×8 ×2-inch buttered baking dish with a layer of zucchini slices. Spoon meat mixture evenly over zucchini and top with remaining slices. Sprinkle with salt and pepper. Cover and bake at 375°F for 25 minutes. Remove cover and top with mozzarella slices and grated Parmesan. Bake 10 minutes longer or until cheese is melted and lightly browned.
Makes 2 servings.

Baked Apples For 2:

Wash and core **2 large baking apples.** Put into a small baking dish and fill center of apples with **brown sugar** and **raisins.** Pour a little water in bottom of dish and dot apples with **butter.** Bake at 375°F 35 minutes. **Makes 2 servings.**

chicken and vegetables

From freezer to oven to table. This one-dish meal for two makes life easy on the cook.

2 broiler chicken quarters, frozen
2 tablespoons lemon juice
1 small clove garlic, pressed
3 tablespoons butter
¼ cup chopped green pepper
1 tablespoon flour
½ cup water
1 chicken bouillon cube
½ cup sherry wine
2 cups frozen hashed brown potatoes
1 cup small whole frozen onions

Defrost broiler quarters enough to separate and spread with lemon juice and garlic. Heat butter and saute green pepper until tender. Stir in flour and add water, bouillon cube and sherry and bring to a boil. Arrange potatoes and onions in a buttered flat 7 ×11-inch metal pan. Put chicken quarters on top and pour sauce over all. Cover and bake at 375°F for about 1 hour. Uncover and bake 15 minutes longer or until nicely browned and chicken is tender. **Makes 2 servings.**

crêpes with chicken stuffing

Chilled cranberry juice to start and a big green salad with tomato wedges to help make this a gala meal. Oven poached pears in wine are a special dessert.

2 tablespoons chopped onion
2 tablespoons butter or margarine
2¹/₂ tablespoons flour
¹/₂ cup dry white wine
³/₄ cup light cream
¹/₂ teaspoon salt
Freshly ground pepper to taste

¹/₄ teaspoon chopped fresh
   tarragon or pinch dried
1¹/₂ cups finely diced cooked
   chicken
8 crêpes*
Parmesan cheese

Sauté onion in butter until tender. Add flour, wine, light cream, salt, pepper and tarragon. Cook and stir until mixture boils. Save ¹/₂ cup of the sauce and add chicken to remainder. Fill crêpes with chicken mixture and roll around filling. Place, seam side down, in a buttered flat casserole large enough to hold crêpes in one layer. Top with reserved sauce and sprinkle with Parmesan. Bake at 400°F for 15 to 20 minutes until browned and bubbly. **Makes 2 servings.**

*A recipe for crêpes can be prepared and frozen. Defrost and use as needed.

Poached Pears In Wine:

Peel **2 ripe pears,** cut in half and remove core. Place in a small casserole and cover with **2 tablespoons lemon juice,** ¹/₂ **cup water,** ¹/₄ **cup sugar,** ¹/₂ **cup ruby port wine** and **peel of** ¹/₂ **orange.** Cover and bake at 400°F for 30 minutes or until tender. Serve warm with a **scoop of ice cream. Makes 2 servings.**

Crêpes:

¹/₂ cup all purpose flour
1 egg
1 egg yolk
¹/₈ teaspoon salt

1 teaspoon sugar
1 cup milk
2 tablespoons corn oil

Combine all ingredients in a bowl and beat with a wire whisk until very smooth. Chill several hours in refrigerator. Oil a 6 or 7-inch skillet and heat over moderate heat. Pour about 2 tablespoons batter into skillet and tilt so that batter covers bottom. Brown on both sides. Remove from skillet and cool on cake rack. Layer crêpes with 2 thicknesses of plastic wrap between each crêpe. Wrap in freezer wrap. Seal, label, date, freeze.

To use:
Defrost crêpes. **Makes 16 crêpes, or 4 servings.**

fish steaks for two

The fish and vegetables take nicely to rice or noodles. Use wedges of crisp let-tuce for salad, and heat some Syrian bread while the fish is cooking.

2 tablespoons melted butter or margarine
Freshly ground pepper to taste
$^1/_8$ teaspoon dried oregano, crushed
1 can (8-ounce) stewed tomatoes
$^1/_2$ can (about 8-ounce) cut green beans
$^1/_2$ teaspoon grated fresh lemon peel
2 teaspoons fresh lemon juice
1 teaspoon sugar
$^3/_4$ to 1 pound fish steaks or fillets cut in 2 serving size pieces
4 tablespoons buttered crumbs

Combine all ingredients except fish and crumbs in an 8 ×8 ×2-inch covered baking dish. Put fish on top of vegetables. If fillets are used, fold so they are at least $^1/_2$-inch thick. Cover and bake at 400°F for 10 minutes. Remove cover, sprinkle fish with crumbs and bake 5 minutes longer, uncovered or until fish flakes easily with a fork. **Makes 2 servings.**

fish rice casserole for one

Here we have combined a fish rice casserole with peas cooked separately in a small casserole and bread heated in the oven. Make some carrot strips and have fresh fruit for dessert.

1 white fleshed fish fillet (about ½ pound) (A piece of codfish, halibut, hake or any local fish will be all right for this recipe.)
¼ cup white wine or water
¾ cup cooked rice
¼ cup chopped celery
2 teaspoons instant minced onion
1 medium tomato, peeled and chopped
½ teaspoon curry powder
Salt and freshly ground pepper to taste
½ cup frozen peas
1 mushroom, optional
Butter or margarine
Salt
3 tablespoons water
Bread, butter

Put wine in a small skillet. Add the fish fillet, cut in two pieces to fit, if necessary. Cover and steam about 5 minutes or until fish flakes easily. If there are any bones, remove. Lightly mix fish and liquid in which it was cooked with rice, celery, instant onion, tomato, curry powder and salt and pepper to taste. Spoon into a buttered 2-cup casserole. Cover. Put peas, 1 sliced mushroom, about a tablespoon of butter or margarine, a little salt and water in a small casserole. Cover. Wrap enough buttered bread for one in foil. It doesn't have to be French or Italian bread. Plain sliced bread buttered and heated in foil tastes mighty good.

To cook:

Bake casserole at 350°F for 30 minutes.
Bake peas at 350°F for 20 minutes.
Bake bread at 350°F for 15 minutes.
Makes 1 serving.

scallops st. jean—dinner for two

A delightful recipe for scallops to be served with the rice and carrots. If it's strawberry time, a bowl for dessert. Other times place defrosted frozen strawberries over vanilla ice cream.

3/4 pound sea scallops
2 tablespoons honey
2 tablespoons soy sauce
3/4 teaspoon curry powder
1 teaspoon lemon juice
1 cup cooked rice
2 tablespoons butter or margarine
2 tablespoons slivered almonds
Salt and freshly ground pepper to taste
1 cup shredded carrots
2 tablespoons raisins
1/4 teaspoon salt
2 tablespoons white wine
2 split, buttered English muffins

Combine scallops with honey, soy sauce, curry powder and lemon juice in a flat metal pan and let stand 30 minutes to 1 hour. Mix rice, butter, almonds and salt and pepper to taste and spoon into a small buttered casserole. Cover. Mix carrots, raisins, 1/4 teaspoon salt and wine and spoon into a small buttered casserole. Cover. To Cook: Remove drip pan and shelf from oven and set other shelf at center position. Preheat oven to "BROIL" or 450°F for 10 minutes. Place casseroles of rice and carrots on shelf. At end of ten minutes, place scallops in pan on rack and split, buttered English Muffins on rack with scallops. Broil 5 to 6 minutes. **Makes 2 servings.**

Cooking With The Kids

The convection oven is perfect for a child's first experience in the kitchen. The big glass door allows for full viewing of items being cooked. Large, easy to set dials pose no problem for little fingers.

Because the convection oven cooks with circulating hot air there are no open flames or radiant heating elements.

The outside of the convection oven stays "touchably cool!" Mothers needn't worry about children burning themselves.

The recipes in this chapter are fun to prepare—and even more fun to eat!

surprise ovenburgers

This is an easy way to make hamburgers and you can make up your own surprise combinations.

8 hamburger buns, split
Butter or margarine

Surprises:

Thin tomato slices
Thin onion slices
¼ slice American cheese
Chili sauce or catsup
Pickle chips
1 pound ground beef

Butter both sides of bun. On bottom half put one of the "surprises." Spread ground beef over "surprise" to cover. Make sure meat covers entire bun (all the way to edge). Preheat oven 10 minutes at "BROIL" or 450°F. Put buns, tops and filled bottoms on cookie sheet and broil for about 5 minutes. Put tops and bottoms together to eat. **Makes 8 buns.**

crazy mixed up beans

Crazy Mixed Up Beans can be an overnight or an all-day slow cooker recipe. Toward the end of the cooking time heat canned brown bread. Cole slaw, fruit and cheese for dessert will make a satisfying meal.

1½ **cups dried pea beans**
1½ **cups dried red kidney beans**
1 cup dried baby lima beans
6 tablespoons molasses
3 teaspoons salt
3 tablespoons prepared mustard
2 cups hot water
½ **pound salt pork**
1 peeled onion

Wash and sort beans and soak overnight in cold water. In the morning bring to a boil and simmer 5 minutes. Drain. Mix molasses, salt and mustard with hot water. Put half of beans in a 2-quart bean pot or casserole. Cut salt pork into 2 pieces and put one piece on top of beans along with onion. Spoon in remaining beans and press remaining salt pork into beans. Add molasses mixture and enough additional hot water to just cover beans. Cover and bake at 225°F for 6 to 7 hours, adding additional water as needed.

Brown Bread:

Remove from can, wrap in aluminum foil and heat for 30 to 40 minutes at 225°F.

granola crunch

A granola recipe will teach the kids what goes into granola. It might also become an economics lesson in comparing the cost of this recipe to a prepared granola.

³/₄ **cup butter or margarine**
¹/₂ **cup preserves (any flavor)**
¹/₄ **cup brown sugar, firmly packed**
3 cups corn bran
1¹/₂ cups uncooked oatmeal
1 teaspoon cinnamon
Dash salt

Combine butter, preserves and sugar in a 1-quart saucepan. Cook and stir over low heat about 5 minutes until well blended. Mix corn bran, oatmeal, cinnamon and salt in a bowl and pour butter mixture over. Stir to coat all cereals. Spread in an even layer in an ungreased 15 ×10-inch jelly roll pan (that means one with sides). Bake at 325°F for 35 minutes or until golden brown, stirring from time to time. Immediately pour baked mixture onto a cookie sheet or a piece of aluminum foil and cool. To store, put in a tightly covered container in a cool dry place or in the refrigerator. Use as a snack or serve over frozen yogurt, ice cream or fruit. **Makes 7 cups.**

chocolate almond ice cream squares

If there are any of the baked squares left over, cut it into finger shaped cookies. It won't last long.

1 square (1-ounce) unsweetened chocolate
¹/₄ **cup butter or margarine**
1 egg
¹/₂ **cup sugar**
¹/₄ **cup all-purpose flour**
¹/₄ **cup diced, roasted almonds**
1 pint (or more) vanilla ice cream
Chocolate sauce

Melt chocolate and butter over very low heat. In a medium bowl, beat egg well. Stir in chocolate mixture, sugar, flour and almonds. Spread into a buttered and floured 8 ×8 ×2-inch pan. Bake at 350°F for 20 minutes. Cool. Cut into squares and serve with vanilla ice cream and chocolate sauce. **Makes 6 to 8 servings.**

cream cheese cookies

These cookies are fun for children to form and dip—but the real fun comes in eating them!

³/₄ **cup shortening**
1 package (3-ounce) cream cheese
³/₄ **cup sugar**
1 egg
1 tablespoon grated orange rind
2¹/₂ **cups all-purpose flour**
¹/₂ **teaspoon salt**
³/₄ **cup chocolate chips, melted**
³/₄ **cup finely chopped walnuts or pecans**

With electric mixer beat shortening, cream cheese and sugar until well blended. Gradually beat in egg, orange rind, flour and salt. Roll dough between hands into ¹/₂×3-inch logs. Place on ungreased cookie sheet about 1-inch apart. Bake at 325°F for 15 to 20 minutes or until browned. Cool. Dip tops of both ends into melted chocolate then into nuts. **Makes 3 dozen.**

Note: A good dough for the cookie press.

mix 'n marble cupcakes

You and the children can make up a batch of these anytime. For a party have the guests frost their own.

2¼ **cups all-purpose flour**
1½ **teaspoons baking powder**
1 teaspoon salt
½ **cup butter or margarine**
1½ **cups sugar**
2 teaspoons vanilla
3 eggs
1 cup milk
1 square (1-ounce) unsweetened chocolate (melted)
Frosting (optional)

Line cupcake tins with papers. In small mixing bowl mix flour, baking powder and salt. Set aside. In a separate mixing bowl beat butter, sugar and vanilla. Add eggs, one at a time, mixing well after each addition. Gradually add milk and flour mixture. Mix at high speed for 3 minutes, scraping down side of bowl if necessary. In mixing bowl place 1½ cups batter. Stir in melted chocolate. Spoon yellow batter and chocolate batter into cupcake papers, filling halfway, marbelizing or alternating layers as desired. Bake at 300°F for 15 to 20 minutes or until cake tester inserted in center comes out clean. Cool. Frost as desired. **Makes 18 to 24 cupcakes.**

Note: When using two racks, bake bottom rack an additional 5 minutes.

christmas ornaments

Use cookie cutters or your imagination to form these inedible "cookies". They'll keep children busy and add sparkle to your holidays.

1 cup salt
2 cups all-purpose flour
¾ **to 1 cup water**

Mix salt and flour in bowl. Gradually add enough water to make a soft dough. Remove dough from bowl and knead 5 to 7 minutes or until smooth. On floured surface roll out ¼-inch thick. Cut with floured cookie cutters, or form into desired shape. Place on lightly greased cookie sheet. Roll small pieces for decorations and press on; cut hole in top for hanging. Bake at 325°F for about 1 hour or until nicely browned. Cool. Paint if desired or spray with varnish. Use old buttons, sequins and beads to add sparkle. Allow to dry before hanging with a piece of yarn or ribbon. **Makes about 12 (3 inch) ornaments.**

Note: Same recipe may be used to make dough baskets, napkin rings, candle holders, braided wreaths, etc.

magic strawberry cake

Children will have a good time watching this cake bake.

1 cup miniature marshmallows
2 cups (two 10-ounce packages) frozen sliced strawberries in
    syrup, completly thawed
1 package (3-ounce) strawberry flavor gelatin
$2\frac{1}{4}$ cups all-purpose flour
$1\frac{1}{2}$ cups sugar
$\frac{1}{2}$ cup shortening
3 teaspoons baking powder
$\frac{1}{4}$ teaspoon salt
1 cup milk
1 teaspoon vanilla extract
3 eggs

Generously grease bottom only of a 13×9-inch baking pan and sprinkle marshmallows evenly over bottom. Combine thawed berries with liquid and gelatin and reserve. In the large bowl of the mixer, combine the remaining ingredients. Beat at low speed until ingredients are moistened and then beat at medium speed for 3 minutes, scraping from side of bowl. Spoon batter over marshmallows and spoon strawberries over batter. Bake at 300°F 45 to 50 minutes or until cake is nicely browned and a toothpick inserted in center comes out clean. Invert cake. Serve warm or cool with ice cream or whipped cream. **Makes 12 to 16 servings.**

friendship loaf

This recipe does not involve a lot of mixing and measuring so children can bake on their own.

¹/₂ cup sugar
2 teaspoons cinnamon
1 loaf frozen yeast bread, partially thawed
Melted butter or margarine
¹/₂ to 1 cup chopped walnuts, pecans or blanched slivered almonds.

Grease 10-inch Bundt pan or angel food cake pan. Mix sugar and cinnamon. Cut bread into 8 to 10 slices and each slice into quarters. Roll each piece into a ball; coat with butter and toss in cinnamon-sugar. Place single layer of balls in prepared pan so they just touch and sprinkle tops with nuts. Repeat with remaining dough and nuts forming second layer. Set temperature to left edge of 150°F setting or between the end of the black line and the 150°F setting. Should feel warm not hot. Let rise until doubled about 1 to 1 ½ hours. Turn to 300°F and bake 25 to 30 minutes or until done. Immediately remove from pan onto serving plate. To serve break apart with fork or fingers.

Note: One tablespoon finely grated orange rind may be used in place of cinnamon.

golden french toast

A delicious hot breakfast that doesn't involve a hot pan over an open flame.

3 eggs, slightly beaten
¹/₄ cup orange juice
¹/₄ cup sugar
Rind from ¹/₄ of an orange, finely grated
6 tablespoons butter or margarine
6 slices white bread, cut in half, diagonally
Powdered sugar

Mix together well the eggs, juice, sugar and grated rind. Set aside. Preheat oven for 10 minutes at "BROIL" or 450°F with rack in center position and drip tray removed. Put butter in drip tray. Set drip tray on rack in oven. When butter has melted, remove tray from oven. Pour egg mixture into a pie plate. Dip pieces of bread in egg mixture and place bread on drip tray. Put drip tray back in oven and bake for 5 to 7 minutes. With pancake turner, turn pieces of bread and bake for 5 to 7 minutes longer. Sprinkle with powdered sugar and serve. **Makes 3 to 4 servings.**

monster cookies

What child wouldn't delight in making a super-sized chocolate chip cookie?

$1/2$ **cup butter or margarine, softened**
$1/2$ **cup sugar**
$1/4$ **cup brown sugar, packed**
1 teaspoon vanilla
1 egg
$1 1/4$ **cups all-purpose flour**
1 teaspoon baking soda
$1/2$ **teaspoon salt**
1 cup semi-sweet chocolate pieces
$1/2$ **cup raisins**

In 2-quart mixing bowl mix butter and sugars until creamy. Add vanilla and beat well. Stir in egg until well blended. Mix in flour, baking soda and salt until stiff dough forms. Add chocolate pieces and raisins. Stir until mixed. Generously grease two 8-inch round cake pans. Spread $1/2$ the dough into each pan covering the surface completely. Bake at 325°F for 20 to 25 minutes. Let cookies cool for five minutes. Gently remove from pan. Cool.
Makes two 8-inch cookies.

menu suggestions

elegant entertaining

Dinner for six
Crown Roast of Lamb (page 32)
Wild Rice Casserole (page 32)
Easy Scalloped Cabbage (page 73)
Mint Jelly
Hot Rolls
Baked Pears in Wine (page 93)

Roast Eye Round with Red Wine
Sauce (page 33)
Broccoli (page 33)
Swedish Potatoes (page 70)
Orange Thins (page 101)
Orange Sherbet

Dinner for Four
Broiled Wild Duck (page 56)
Casserole of Noodles and Cottage Cheese
(page 56)
Steamed Vegetables
Apple Torte Pie (page 106)

Wine Marinated Steak (page 35)
Escalloped Corn and Tomatoes (page 76)
Sour Cream Onion Squares (page 72)
Lemon Cake Ring (page 108)

Dinner for Two
Crêpes with Chicken Stuffing (page 127)
Asparagus Spears
Easy Brownie Pie (page 107)

Fish Steaks for Two (page 128)
Double Corn Bread (page 80)
Danish Pound Cake (page 109)

brunch

Orange Juice
Hot Cross Buns (page 81)
Mushroom Cheese Souffle (page 16)
Coffee   Tea

Lobster Quiche (page 57)
Tossed Greens
Honey Rice Pudding (page 97)
Coffee   Tea

Salmon Mushroom Loaf (page 59)
Brioche (page 82)
Tropical Baked Bananas (page 93)

hearty fall suppers

Homemade Chicken Pie (page 54)
Twice Baked Sweet Potatoes (page 69)
Cranberry Apple Crisp (page 95)

Hearty Beef Soup (page 46)
Easy Cheese Bread (page 86)
Corn Pudding (page 76)
Baked Spiced Applesauce
(page 94)

Pork Ribs and Sauerkraut (page 45)
Baked Squash Casserole (page 66)
Whole Wheat French Bread (page 83)

summer specials

Kebabs (page 36)
Endive and Mushroom Salad
Baked Cherry Short Cake (page 107)

Barbecue Spareribs (page 42)
Baked Potatoes
Artichoke Hearts
Whole Wheat Walnut Cookies (page 102)
Ice Cream

Broiled Wine Burgers (page 34)
Twice Baked Potatoes (page 71)
Mixed Green Salad
Broiled Grapefruit Halves (page 97)

As the United States adopts the metric system, people will need to learn new units of measurement. The following chart can be used to change your recipe to metrics.

metric conversion chart

WEIGHT

Multiply ounces × 28 to get grams   gm
Multiply pounds × 0.45 to get kilograms   kg

VOLUME

Multiply teaspoons	× 5	to get milliliters	ml
Multiply tablespoons	× 15	to get milliliters	ml
Multiply ounces	× 30	to get milliliters	ml
Multiply cups	× 0.24	to get liters	l
Multiply pints	× 0.47	to get liters	l
Multiply quarts	× 0.95	to get liters	l
Multiply gallons	× 3.8	to get liters	l

TEMPERATURE

To change from Fahrenheit to Celsius:
    Subtract 32 from Fahrenheit, divide by 9 and multiply by 5. This will give you the Celsius. In Celsius, freezing is 0°—in Fahrenheit it is 32°.
To change from Celsius to Fahrenheit:
    Multiply Celsius by 9 and divide by 5 and add 32.

index